Gangs

OTHER BOOKS OF RELATED INTEREST

Gangs

J.D. Lloyd, *Book Editor*

Daniel Leone, *President*
Bonnie Szumski, *Publisher*
Scott Barbour, *Managing Editor*

Contemporary Issues
Companion

GREENHAVEN PRESS
SAN DIEGO, CALIFORNIA

GALE GROUP
™
THOMSON LEARNING
Detroit • New York • San Diego • San Francisco
Boston • New Haven, Conn. • Waterville, Maine
London • Munich

Every effort has been made to trace the owners of copyrighted material. The articles in this volume may have been edited for content, length, and/or reading level. The titles have been changed to enhance the editorial purpose. Those interested in locating the original source will find the complete citation on the first page of each article.

No part of this book may be reproduced or used in any form or by any means, electrical, mechanical, or otherwise, including, but not limited to, photocopy, recording, or any information storage and retrieval system, without prior written permission from the publisher.

Library of Congress Cataloging-in-Publication Data

Gangs / J.D. Lloyd, book editor.
        p. cm. — (Contemporary issues companion)
    Includes bibliographical references and index.
    ISBN 0-7377-0830-1 (pbk. : alk. paper) —
ISBN 0-7377-0831-X (lib. : alk. paper)
        1. Gangs—United States. 2. Juvenile delinquency—United States.
I. Lloyd, J.D., 1959–   . II. Series (Unnumbered)

CONTENTS

FOREWORD

In the news, on the streets, and in neighborhoods, individuals are confronted with a variety of social problems. Such problems may affect people directly: A young woman may struggle with depression, suspect a friend of having bulimia, or watch a loved one battle cancer. And even the issues that do not directly affect her private life—such as religious cults, domestic violence, or legalized gambling—still impact the larger society in which she lives. Discovering and analyzing the complexities of issues that encompass communal and societal realms as well as the world of personal experience is a valuable educational goal in the modern world.

Effectively addressing social problems requires familiarity with a constantly changing stream of data. Becoming well informed about today's controversies is an intricate process that often involves reading myriad primary and secondary sources, analyzing political debates, weighing various experts' opinions—even listening to first-hand accounts of those directly affected by the issue. For students and general observers, this can be a daunting task because of the sheer volume of information available in books, periodicals, on the evening news, and on the Internet. Researching the consequences of legalized gambling, for example, might entail sifting through congressional testimony on gambling's societal effects, examining private studies on Indian gaming, perusing numerous websites devoted to Internet betting, and reading essays written by lottery winners as well as interviews with recovering compulsive gamblers. Obtaining valuable information can be time-consuming—since it often requires researchers to pore over numerous documents and commentaries before discovering a source relevant to their particular investigation.

Greenhaven's Contemporary Issues Companion series seeks to assist this process of research by providing readers with useful and pertinent information about today's complex issues. Each volume in this anthology series focuses on a topic of current interest, presenting informative and thought-provoking selections written from a wide variety of viewpoints. The readings selected by the editors include such diverse sources as personal accounts and case studies, pertinent factual and statistical articles, and relevant commentaries and overviews. This diversity of sources and views, found in every Contemporary Issues Companion, offers readers a broad perspective in one convenient volume.

In addition, each title in the Contemporary Issues Companion series is designed especially for young adults. The selections included in every volume are chosen for their accessibility and are expertly edited in consideration of both the reading and comprehension levels of the audience. The structure of the anthologies also enhances accessibility. An introductory essay places each issue in context and provides helpful facts such as historical background or current statistics and legislation that pertain to the topic. The chapters that follow organize the material and focus on specific aspects of the book's topic. Every essay is introduced by a brief summary of its main points and biographical information about the author. These summaries aid in comprehension and can also serve to direct readers to material of immediate interest and need. Finally, a comprehensive index allows readers to efficiently scan and locate content.

The Contemporary Issues Companion series is an ideal launching point for research on a particular topic. Each anthology in the series is composed of readings taken from an extensive gamut of resources, including periodicals, newspapers, books, government documents, the publications of private and public organizations, and Internet websites. In these volumes, readers will find factual support suitable for use in reports, debates, speeches, and research papers. The anthologies also facilitate further research, featuring a book and periodical bibliography and a list of organizations to contact for additional information.

A perfect resource for both students and the general reader, Greenhaven's Contemporary Issues Companion series is sure to be a valued source of current, readable information on social problems that interest young adults. It is the editors' hope that readers will find the Contemporary Issues Companion series useful as a starting point to formulate their own opinions about and answers to the complex issues of the present day.

INTRODUCTION

On September 17, 1995, a family car took a wrong turn onto a dead-end street in the Cypress Park section of Los Angeles. When the driver stopped to turn the car around, local gang members opened fire with automatic weapons, riddling the vehicle with bullets. As the car sped away, the driver's three-year-old daughter was shot in the head and killed. The driver and his two-year-old son were also wounded.

This tragic event is characteristic of the senseless violence that marks modern gang activity. Although gang members have traditionally engaged in violence, in the past they mostly harmed rival gangsters. Increasingly, however, their victims include random passersby and others unlucky enough to be caught in the wrong place at the wrong time. Researchers agree that over the past few decades, gang violence has not only increased in frequency, but also escalated in lethality. In their book *Juvenile Gangs*, Herbert C. Covey, Scott Menard, and Robert J. Franzese note:

> The nature of gang violence has evolved from small-scale confrontations and the rare but impressive large-scale "rumbles" of the 1950s and 1960s into the more frequent and more heavily armed guerilla forays, gang-bangs, and drive-by shootings of the 1980s and 1990s.

Sociologists have identified several factors associated with the rise in gang violence. One component is the growing availability of guns. During the 1950s and 1960s, gang violence was most likely to involve fistfights or stabbings. As researcher Lewis Yablonsky writes in his book *Gangsters: Fifty Years of Madness, Drugs, and Death on the Streets of America*, the use of guns was uncommon during this era:

> Manufactured handguns were seldom used in gang warfare, and there were no automatic weapons on the street. Occasionally, a zip gun would be employed in a gang fight. . . . This unreliable weapon was comprised of a metal pipe as a barrel, a wooden handle, and a bunch of heavy elastic bands to provide the power to shoot a bullet. When the trigger was pulled . . . , the bullet was as likely to shoot the shooter as the intended target.

Zip guns pale in comparison with the brutally efficient firearms of choice in the present day: automatic assault weapons such as the Uzi, the AK-47, and the MAC-10, which are capable of firing over twenty rounds of ammunition in the span of a few seconds. Modern gangsters regularly use these firearms in drive-by shootings to spray bullets at as many rivals as possible. Unfortunately, innocent bystanders often become unintentional victims. According to Yablonsky,

> various research, including police reports, reveals that only
> about 50 percent of gang-related murders hit the target of
> enemy gangsters. The other 50 percent of victims of gangster
> drive-bys and street violence are innocent children and adults
> who happen to be at the wrong place at the wrong time.

Guns have become status symbols for modern gangsters—particularly for "wannabes" who are seeking to advance in the gang hierarchy—and gun ownership among gang members has risen sharply in recent years. For instance, in the short eight-year span from 1985 to 1993, the Bureau of Justice reported a 100 percent increase in the number of juveniles arrested for weapons offenses. Gang members obtain their guns primarily through the illegal weapons trade on the street or by burglarizing homes and businesses. As guns become commonplace in gang neighborhoods, they are used more routinely to settle disputes or inflame turf wars. Modern gangsters, assuming that their rivals are armed, often answer the slightest insult with gunfire.

The increase in gang involvement with drugs has also been a factor in the escalation of gang violence. During the 1960s and 1970s, changes in the economy led many gang members to enter the drug-trafficking business. As researcher Irving A. Spergel notes, "changing labor market conditions . . . , especially the decrease of low-skilled manufacturing jobs, made it difficult for older gang youths to find legitimate employment and leave the teenage gang." Instead, these older gangsters turned to illegal ways of making money, most often selling drugs. The successful drug dealers evolved into drug czars within their gangs, employing lower-ranking gang members as "mules" to deliver their products.

The issue of territory became increasingly important as rival gangs sought to establish their presence on the street as drug salesmen. Inevitably, disputes turned violent, and drug-dealing gang members quickly gained a reputation for being willing to murder on a whim. In 1988, a New York City special narcotics prosecutor explained:

> These gangs are more violent than anything this city has ever
> experienced. Crack cocaine has spawned an allied industry of
> young hit men who kill for the slightest reasons. In 1958 it
> took only 11 homicides in an outbreak of gang mayhem with
> zip guns and knives to stun the city. Recently, in northern
> Manhattan alone, . . . drug gangs have been responsible for as
> many as 500 gang-related murders.

This type of drug-related violence is not limited to big cities. For example, in the summer of 1994, the relatively small Los Angeles neighborhood of Venice witnessed twenty-two gang-related murders, mostly involving disputes over drug-selling turf. The random and cold-blooded nature of drug-related gang killings leaves neighbor-hood residents feeling terrified. Many hide in their own homes to avoid getting caught in the crossfire of a drug deal gone bad.

Drug-related gang violence took a new turn in 1995 when a Boston prosecutor—known for his pursuit of inner-city gangsters—was gunned down on the street by a hooded teenager believed to be associated with a gang. At the time of his death, he was in the process of prosecuting several Boston gangs on drug charges. News reports likened the killing to the types of assassinations carried out by the Mafia or the drug cartels of Colombia.

Turf is another factor related to the rise in gang violence. Most gang members grow up in neighborhoods blighted by poor economic, social, and environmental conditions. Ironically, belonging to the "hood" provides gangsters with one of their few securities in life—one which they are quick to defend. Researcher James Vigil quotes a young gang member regarding the relationship of territory to violence:

> The only thing we can do is build our own little nation. We know that we have complete control in our community. It's like we're making our stand. . . . We take pride in our little nation and if any intruders enter, we get panicked because we feel our community is being threatened. The only way [to respond] is with violence.

In past decades, gangs were associated with the neighborhoods in which their members resided. Battles usually erupted over disputed borderlines or when one gang member forayed into the territory of another gang. Modern gangs, however, have expanded their turf to include schools, shopping malls, and other public areas not necessarily within a particular neighborhood. Territories can also be fluid, changing with whichever gangsters happen to occupy a certain space at a certain time. This wider and unstable definition of turf has drastically heightened the chances of violent conflict breaking out between opposing gangs and has made it more likely that such violence will occur in public areas filled with innocent bystanders.

Whether gang members or not, teenagers often travel in fear within the increasingly complex web of gang territories. The association of certain colors and types of clothing with specific gangs—accompanied by the growing tendency of gang members to shoot first and ask questions later—has made it dangerous for teens who are not affiliated with gangs to pass through gang-controlled territories. For example, in the early 1990s, the Cleveland Task Force on Violent Crime noted that "kids began riding buses with clothes-filled book bags 12 months of the year so that they could change their clothes between gang turfs to travel safely through other neighborhoods." Their fear was not unfounded. In 1988, a teenager was gunned down while riding his bike through a gang-controlled neighborhood in

Denver, Colorado. Wearing a baseball cap of a color associated with one of two local rival gangs, he was apparently mistaken by a gang member for an enemy gangster.

Such random shootings have increasingly made gang violence a problem not just for gang members but for the general public as well. The violent nature of modern gangs is only one of the pressing issues examined in *Gangs: Contemporary Issues Companion*. The chapters that follow explore the history of gangs, the expanding identity of modern gangs, and the realities of life in a gang. The causes of gang involvement and measures designed to reduce and prevent gang activity are also discussed. The articles included in this anthology present a broad range of voices: experts in sociology and criminal justice, social workers, law enforcement agencies, educators, journalists, and past and present gang members. While not offering any pat answers, these authors provide a wide variety of perspectives on this increasingly important social problem.

CHAPTER 1

THE HISTORY OF GANGS

EARLY TWENTIETH-CENTURY GANG PRECURSORS

Lewis Yablonsky

A retired professor of sociology and criminology at California State University in Northridge, Lewis Yablonsky has spent much of his academic career studying gangs. He is the author of fifteen books, including *The Violent Gang*. In the following excerpt from his book *Gangsters: Fifty Years of Madness, Drugs, and Death on the Streets of America*, Yablonsky traces the early development of gangs from the adult gangs of turn-of-the-century New York to the organized crime gangs of the Roaring Twenties. He also examines the pre-1950s youth gangs that were the direct precursors of modern gangs.

Juvenile gangs emerged over the years from a mold created by early adult gangs. The earliest reports of adult gangs in America appear around the turn of the twentieth century on the Lower East Side of New York City. The phenomenon was chronicled in a colorful 1928 book by Herbert Asbury called *Gangs of New York*.

These early gangs had such names as the Dusters, the Pug Uglies, the Dead Rabbits, and the notorious Five Points gangs. According to Asbury, the Five Points gangs and the Bowery gangs carried out their grudges against each other with constant warfare. Scarcely a week passed without a half dozen conflicts. On one occasion, led by the Dead Rabbits and the Pug Uglies, all of the gangs of the Five Points began their celebration of the Fourth of July with a raid on the clubhouse building of the Bowery Boys and the Atlantic Guards gangs. There was furious fighting, but the Bowery gangsters triumphed and drove their enemies back to their own neighborhood. In the melee, a few metropolitan policemen who tried to interfere with the gang warfare were badly beaten. There were apparently no guns or knives used. The warfare took the form of fistfighting and the use of a few bats.

Characteristics of Early Adult Gangs

The gangs of this era were territorial, and this factor may have set the precedent for the enormous value placed on turf, hood, and barrio by contemporary youth gangs. Another factor in the early adult gangs that may have set a precedent for today's gangs was a disrespect and antipathy toward the police. If anything, the gangs of that era were more hostile toward "the coppers" (so-called because of their copper badges) than contemporary gangs. Disrespect for the police, therefore, as representatives of the larger society who were intruding on gang turf, began at the turn of the century.

Asbury describes how the police ineffectually responded to an early gang fight:

> A lone policeman, with more courage than judgment, tried to club his way through the mass of struggling men and arrest the ringleaders, but he was knocked down, his clothing stripped from his body, and he was fearfully beaten with his own nightstick. He crawled through the plunging mob to the sidewalk, and, naked except for a pair of cotton drawers, ran to the Metropolitan headquarters in White street, where he gasped out the alarm and collapsed. A squad of policemen was dispatched to stop the rioting, but when they marched bravely up Center street the gangs made common cause against them, and they were compelled to retreat after a bloody encounter in which several policemen were injured.

These early gang wars bear some resemblance to current gang battles: They were territorially divided, and gang members didn't shrink from violence in their encounters. However, the extent to which battles involved large numbers of adult citizens, no guns, and the lack of police control shows an apparent difference from modern gang wars. The formal police framework of control and direct gang suppression is, of course, stronger today. Another significant differential between these early gangs and today's gangs is the absence of the lucrative commerce of drugs. Also, these early gang wars were not nearly as lethal as today's conflicts, largely because of the absence of today's prevalence of guns and automatic weapons in the hands of the combatants.

There are also data that seem to suggest that the current violent gangs have a more pathological "membership" than the earlier forms. The early gangs appeared to be socially acceptable group structures, at least within the norms and values of the neighborhood in which they existed. Although most of the public may have considered the gang's behavior deviant, it was normal in the particular neighborhood in which it occurred. Senseless, unprovoked gangbanging for kicks and ego gratification did not seem to be part of the early gangs' pattern. However, the criminal social fabric of illegal liquor sales, theft, and particularly politics was closely integrated with the gang activity of that era.

A new era of adult gang violence was ushered in by the bootleg gangs of the Roaring Twenties. In a way they set the precedent for today's gangs and their involvement in the commerce of illegal drugs. The deviant gangster culture and its practice of drive-by murders was created and developed in this violent era in America, as was its romanticization.

In carrying out research for a biography I wrote about the movie actor George Raft, I interviewed Howard Hawks, who directed the original *Scarface,* one of the best films on 1920s gangster behavior. Hawks's film was largely based on the criminal gang exploits of Al Capone. This was the first film that depicted the newly invented drive-by gangster murders of that era. Hawks told me that in doing research for this film he interviewed gangsters from Chicago, members of the Capone mob who had actually carried out drive-by murders in the 1920s. The gangster drive-by, a unique American invention, was created and developed by Al Capone. Hawks informed me,

> Originally I had one drive-by murder scene in *Scarface.* This opened the film. When my producer Howard Hughes saw this, at that time, strange vehicle method for murder, he asked me how prevalent this practice was in gangland. I told him it was used as a standard practice for killing enemy gangsters. Hughes then told me, "Put more of those dramatic drive-by scenes in the movie."

A Part of Society

These early bootleg gangs, although illegal, were not alien to the society in which they existed. Despite their bloody intergang and intra-gang murders, they maintained a close affiliation with the political, social, and economic conditions of the times. The gangsters of the twenties were the henchmen of political maneuverers and some of the big businessmen of that period. Gangsters were used in management-labor conflicts and to control liquor sales, prostitution, and gambling.

Violence was used as an instrument of establishing and maintaining these somewhat socially accepted business ventures. Capone called these enterprises "the legitimate rackets," and his self-concept was that of a businessman providing needed services for his community. Many community leaders, politicians, and citizens supported these early gangs.

The pre-Prohibition gangs of New York were usually classified by their national, religious, or racial background. They were principally made up of newly arrived groups like the Irish, Italians, and Jews. Irish gangs controlled the West Side, and the East Side belonged to the Italian and the Jewish gangs. The Lower East Side of Manhattan in the first twenty years of the century was the breeding ground for many gunmen and racketeers. In a subtle way, through movie and news reports, the Vito Genoveses, Lucky Lucianos, Bugsy Siegels, Meyer Lanskys, and Frank Costellos that emerged in those days became the role models for today's gangsters.

Italy's major criminal export to America in this period was the "mafia," or "crime syndicate." Its early form in the United States was the secret order of the Unione Siciliane, often referred to as the Black Hand. This early form of La Cosa Nostra originated in this country through a leader known as Ignazio (Lupo the Wolf). The Unione had several local bosses until Joe "the Boss" Masseria took charge in the 1920s. The Unione at that time was not restricted to gangsters. Among its members were some men of respectable reputations and occupations. Occasionally the doors to membership were opened to non-Italians such as lawyers who performed the helpful job of acquitting some Unione gangster in the courts.

The early form of joining a gang allegedly involved a ritual of initiation that included an ancient rite of scratching the wrist of the initiate and the wrists of the members, after which an exchange of blood was effected by laying the wounds one on the other, thus making them all blood brothers. Many people have seen this ritual aggrandized in such films as *The Godfather* and *Goodfellas*. This was an early form of what today's gangbangers call the jumping-in ritual, but being jumped-in is a more bloody procedure since the worthy initiate is often brutally beaten by his homie gangsters.

Routine Murders

As part of the normal business of the various illicit enterprises conducted by the gangs of the twenties, homicide was employed as a logical, important, and normal activity for the enforcement of gang rules. Several thousand gangsters died in New York and Chicago in the bootleg liquor wars of the 1920s over disputes related to the operation of the illegal liquor business. Sometimes, but not as often as today's gangs, the drive-bys killed innocent victims.

The murder of a bootlegger became a daily event. Rumrunners and hijackers were pistol-whipped and machine gunned. They were taken for rides on the front seats of sedans, garroted from behind, and at times had their brains blown out with a bullet to the back of the head by fellow mobsters they thought were their pals. They were lined up in pairs in front of warehouse walls in lonely alleys and shot down by enemy-gang firing squads. They were slugged into unconsciousness and placed in burlap sacks with their hands, feet, and necks so roped that they would strangle themselves as they writhed. Charred bodies were found in bombed automobiles. Bootleggers and sometimes their molls were pinioned with wire and dropped alive into the East River. Others were encased in cement and tossed overboard from rum boats in the harbor. In a way, gang murders of this early era were more inventive than today's gangsters.

Life was cheap and murder was easy in the bootleg industry; the early gangsters who fought their way to the top were endowed with savagery and shrewdness. The killings were carried out to consolidate gang territory for greater illicit profit. Murders were not usually committed for emotional reasons but were part of cold and calculated gang business practices. In some cases, former gang friends killed their friends with a comment like, "Listen Charlie, I like you, this is nothing personal—it's just business." And often the victim would quietly cooperate with his own demise by saying, "I understand."

Calculated Killers

The form of these gang-war murders was different than today's violent gang murders; however, the lethal results were similar. Although contemporary gangs engaged in the commerce of drugs carry out hits against rivals who invade their territory, their violence is not as precise as the earlier form of gang murders. The enforcers of the earlier gangs killed in a businesslike fashion. Their personal kicks and distorted ego gratifications, unlike modern gangs, were secondary to their professional demands.

This early type of calculated murder by a violent gangster is depicted in the career of the infamous mob hitman Abe "Kid Twist" Reles. Reles admitted committing over eighty murders in the normal course of his work as an agent of New York's Murder, Inc., a division of the Meyer Lansky/Bugsy Siegal gang. According to all reports, the murders that Reles committed had an unemotional quality. Reles claimed that he never committed a murder out of passion, excitement, jealousy, personal revenge, or any of the usual motives. He killed impersonally and solely for business considerations.

Early gangsters, like Reles, were not allowed to kill on their own initiative. Murders were ordered by the leaders at the top on behalf of the welfare of the organization. A member of the mob who would dare kill on his own initiative or for his personal passion or profit would often be executed. Organized crime murders were a business matter organized by the chiefs in conference and carried out in a disciplined and efficient way.

Expanding Influence

When Prohibition was abolished, the early criminal gangs with their great wealth earned from bootlegging and other illegal enterprises entered into more legitimate rackets. They developed quasi-legitimate businesses by controlling unions, government building contracts, refuse removal services, and extortion from legitimate businesses. They eliminated competition through violence. They were exposed in the 1950s and 1960s by the Senate Kefauver committee and later on by Attorney General Robert Kennedy's war on organized crime.

The mob to this day earns billions of dollars from racketeering, extortion, the commerce of drugs, and other illegal enterprises. A large source of mob money for investment in illegal and to some

extent legal business activities has come from the mob's hidden ownership of Las Vegas casinos. The gambling business, legal in Nevada,
has produced billions of dollars legally and through money-skimming
activities from the casinos of mob owned or controlled hotels.

These billions have been funneled into the coffers of organized
crime bosses and troops. Along the way over the past fifty years, the
mob's activities and internecine conflicts have resulted in thousands
of murders; there are hundreds of unmarked graves in the deserts of
Nevada. A semifictionalized version of these gang activities appeared
in the film *Casino*. These murders, for business and profit, parallel
some of the murders committed in the past ten years by the new
form of the violent–drug gangs fighting over drug territory on the
streets of America.

Many contemporary gang murders have a drug business motivation; however, the emotion-driven gangbanging form of territorial
protection violence remains a part of the violence committed by
today's gangs. Most of the contemporary gangster drive-by murders,
in contrast to the 1920's drive-bys, are motivated by an emotional
paranoid revenge factor, either real or imagined, rather than for drug
business purposes. They typically involve a group of gangsters, high
on drugs or alcohol, who are full of rage at the world and go on a
senseless murderous foray into what they perceive is enemy territory.
After announcing their presence with the verbal gang sign of "Hey
cuz," they may blow away with an Uzi or an AK 47 several children or
older family members having a picnic in their backyard along with
their intended enemy gangsters.

Pre-1950 Youth Gangs

Contemporary violent youth gangs have a historical precedent not
only in adult gangs but also in earlier forms of youth groups. The
term "youth gang" has been used for a variety of diverse youth
groupings significantly different from the current violent drug gangs.
The generic term "gang" to describe youth collectivities in the early
part of the twentieth century has been applied to collections of
youths organized to go fishing, to play baseball, to steal cars, or to
commit homicide.

One of the earliest applications of the term "gang" to youth
groups was made by Henry D. Sheldon in 1898. He classified gangs,
according to their activities, as (1) secret clubs, (2) predatory organizations, (3) social clubs, (4) industrial associations, (5) philanthropic
associations, (6) literary and musical organizations, and (7) athletic
clubs. He maintained at the time that, among boys' clubs, "the athletic clubs are immensely the most popular, with predatory organizations a poor second."

An early description and use of the term "gang" was presented in J.
Adams Puffer's 1905 publication entitled "Boy Gangs." Puffer's gangs

were essentially boys' clubs and athletic teams. He described one early gang's activity as follows:

> We met out in the woods back of an old barn on Spring Street. Met every day if we did not get work. Any fellow could bring in a fellow if others approved. Put a fellow out for spying or telling anything about the club. Tell him we didn't want him and then if he didn't take the hint force him out. We played ball; went swimming, fishing, and shooting. Each of us had a rifle. Meet (at night) and tell stories of what we had done during the day. . . . The purpose of club was to steal; most anything we could get our hands on; fruit from fruit stands; ice cream at picnics, and rob stores. . . . Especially noteworthy is the desire of the gang for a local habitation, its own special street corner, its club room, its shanty in the woods.

Early youth gang researchers and writers seldom used any complex theoretical categories for describing the gangs they studied. Essentially they relied on descriptive appraisals—presenting the gang, so to speak, as is, based on their firsthand observations. More recent students of gang behavior have utilized more abstract analyses, including computerized statistical analyses.

THE IMPACT OF WORLD WAR II ON GANGS

Eric C. Schneider

Eric C. Schneider is a history professor and the assistant dean of the College of Arts and Sciences at the University of Pennsylvania. In the following excerpt from his book *Vampires, Dragons, and Egyptian Kings: Youth Gangs in Postwar New York*, Schneider asserts that the period of World War II was seminal in the development of youth gangs. Schneider illustrates how the wartime economy provided many young people with the financial independence to challenge adult authority. Furthermore, he explains, racial tensions intensified during this era as African Americans and Latinos moved into traditionally white neighborhoods, and these tensions were often mirrored in hostilities between youth gangs of different ethnic composition. Although public officials initially dismissed the problem, increasingly violent conflicts in neighborhoods experiencing ethnic transition finally made gangs impossible to ignore, Schneider concludes.

World War II marked a turning point in the discovery of the youth gang, although this occurred gradually and in three phases. First, public authorities discovered the problem of youth. Adolescents flaunted their independence from adult authority and participated in nightlife and commercial pleasures, as a superheated wartime economy absorbed their labor and supplied them with disposable income. Police rushed to reassert control over wayward youth, and rapidly increasing adolescent arrest rates made juvenile delinquency a topic of national debate during the war. Second, the race riots of 1943 linked the issues of ethnicity, youth, and violence. In Los Angeles, Detroit, New York, and other cities across the nation, African Americans, Latinos, and Euro-Americans battled over the color line. Usually young men were in the forefront in these disorders, which fueled concerns about out-of-control youth. A debate over race, youth, and crime initially ignored gangs, but finally, clashes in New York neighborhoods undergoing ethnic succession made gangs impossible to overlook any longer. First residents and then municipal authorities came to recognize their existence as a major social problem.

Commentators blamed increasing youth problems on "wartime conditions." With family life disrupted as older men joined the military and women moved into the workforce, stories abounded of "latchkey children" left on their own or with adolescents who handled adult responsibilities with varying degrees of effectiveness. Migration separated some families as men searched for defense employment, or it threatened to overwhelm boomtown communities and established neighborhoods as migrant families poured in. Even more problematic than rootless adults were the scores of rootless youths, able to free themselves of institutional and familial restraints.

Concern about adolescent behavior initially focused on girls. In the past, female delinquency had been defined largely in terms of sexual activity, and little had changed by World War II. Newspaper headlines warned of fourteen- or fifteen-year-old "Victory Girls" who exhibited their patriotism by picking up soldiers in dance halls, train stations, or on the streets. Girls, rather than their male partners, were blamed for the rising venereal disease rate, which sapped soldiers' health and delayed their military deployment. Prevention focused on controlling female delinquents, and their delinquency remained an issue of paramount importance throughout the war.

Adolescent males who exercised adult prerogatives and threatened to overturn the hierarchy of age and class were another concern. Working-class males, including Euro-Americans, African Americans, Puerto Ricans, and, in the West, Mexican Americans, had money and entered the public spaces of downtown entertainment districts. These young men enjoyed a peculiar freedom that contrasted strikingly with the constraints placed on a wartime society. They had entered a liminal [threshold] stage, not yet adults but no longer children, newly freed from the tyranny of school but not yet fully incorporated into the discipline of work, awaiting word of draft status, newly affluent with their wartime paychecks, and able to participate in the culture of poolrooms, juke joints, dance halls, and all-night movie houses. . . . The mixture of relative affluence, uncertainty, and independence led to adult anxiety.

The zoot suit became the most famous emblem of independent working-class youth. Latino, African-American, and Euro-American males employed the hip jive talk of the jazz world, plunged into the pleasures of the nighttime entertainment districts, jitterbugged, and wore zoot suits—outrageously flamboyant badges of youthful freedom. Zoot suits mocked somber military uniforms with their bright pastel colors and defied warnings of wartime shortages with their long coats, broadly padded shoulders, and voluminous pleats. . . .

Most important, the zoot suit, while remembered as a form of dress favored by African-American and Latino youth, transcended ethnicity.

At a time when African-American and Latino migrants poured into still-segregated cities, the zoot suit represented racial transgression for whites. Its wearing did not symbolize tolerance, however, as zoot-suited gangs still organized along ethnic lines. Rather, Euro-American adolescents appropriated African-American and Latino cultural forms—including bebop and the zoot suit—as the most provocative way of expressing both the joy of consumption after the long dry years of the Depression and their rebellion against parents, school, employers, and their impending incorporation into the war effort. Young African Americans employed the zoot suit to celebrate a bebop-based culture, reject the color line, and express opposition to the war. . . . This sort of overt rebelliousness, symbolized in the styles of adolescent dress, aroused a response on the part of authorities and the public at large.

To gain control over adolescent behavior, police began arresting larger and larger numbers of youths. The Federal Bureau of Investigation reported that arrests of girls under twenty-one had increased by 55 percent between 1941 and 1942, in response to the hysteria over adolescent girls cruising for soldiers. Boys also had their activities checked, with juvenile courts reporting as much as a one-third increase in their caseloads of delinquent boys between 1942 and 1943. That many offenses were comparatively minor did not seem to matter. FBI director J. Edgar Hoover maintained that the surging juvenile crime rate threatened the stability of the nation. In New York City, the press began a sensationalized campaign about African-American crime following the murder of a fifteen-year-old white youth by three black adolescents in the fall of 1941. Story after story focused on the "Harlem crime wave," in which many of the perpetrators were young males, and these accounts merged into the coverage of increasing wartime delinquency. Of all wartime phenomena, juvenile behavior was the most susceptible to control, and as a result, juvenile arrest rates soared. The wartime juvenile crime wave was produced as much by the effort to curb youthful behavior as by the growth of misbehavior itself.

Gangs formed a comparatively minor part of this overall picture. The Office of War Information (OWI) reported that adolescents, envious of the adventures of their older brothers and male relatives, had formed "commando gangs" that imitated military tactics, stole weapons, and initiated raids into enemy territory. The OWI also alleged that gangs were responsible for acts of theft, arson, and vandalism, but, surprisingly its report still did not take gangs very seriously. The influence of the prewar gang boy studies is readily apparent. Federal officials continued to see gangs simply as boys' play groups that had gotten a bit out of hand.

Interethnic clashes, beginning with the Los Angeles zoot suit riots of June 1943, were the second step in the process of discovering gangs. The zoot suit riots—actually attacks by Euro-Americans on

Mexican-American youth—followed several months of tension between white servicemen and Mexican-American "pachucos" [flashily dressed youths]. A number of servicemen had been mugged after leaving bars or while looking for sexual liaisons with Mexican-American women, and in the zoot suit riots they gained revenge. Soldiers, painfully aware of their impending shipment overseas, no doubt resented the freedom enjoyed by their rivals. Aided by civilians, they attacked Mexican-American youths, stripping them of their zoot suits, beating them up, and ritualistically cutting off their ducktails. The turmoil lasted for ten days until the military finally declared downtown Los Angeles off limits to servicemen.

Even though zoot-suited adolescents were the victims, not the perpetrators of violence, the riots reinforced an image of minority youth as criminal. Even the way they were discussed, as "zoot suit riots," erased the role of Euro-American servicemen in the conflict and focused only on the disorder of minority youth. The Los Angeles City Council considered a resolution making wearing a zoot suit a misdemeanor but finally decided that existing legislation on disorderly conduct sufficed to control Mexican-American youth. Newspapers, such as the New York Times, followed the lead of Los Angeles authorities and began to comment on the style of youthful troublemakers. The paper referred to "zoot-suit gangs" that engaged in thievery, fighting, and knifings and noted in local news stories when criminals wore zoot suits. The Times stories associated a certain style and young males—especially African Americans and Puerto Ricans—with crime and rebelliousness.

These issues were brought home for New Yorkers later that same summer with the Harlem riot of 1943. The immediate cause of the Harlem riot was the rumored shooting by a white police officer of an African-American serviceman protecting his mother. Although the facts of the case were somewhat different, the rumor seemed credible because of accounts of police brutality and a series of shootings in Harlem, in which plainclothes police officers acted as decoys and then shot their would-be muggers. Harlemites' anger at police abuse, at discrimination, at their higher rents for shoddier apartments, and at the color line in general exploded in attacks on white-owned stores and on police.

Young African-American males were leading participants in the looting and destruction that accompanied the riot. Author Claude Brown, who at the time was the child "mascot" of a gang called the Buccaneers, recalled the turmoil that accompanied the riot. When he went outside the morning after the riot, he did not recognize his neighborhood. Glass from shattered store windows littered the street, stores had been broken into, and a virtual army of police occupied Harlem. Despite the police presence, Brown and his friends took the opportunity to raid local stores for food on what was perhaps one of the few occasions

when any Harlemite could have a full larder. Another youthful partici-
pant in the riot, "R" (clad, the interviewer noted, in a zoot suit),
described more serious violence that occurred farther uptown, where
Harlem met a Euro-American community in Washington Heights, and
where young men could attack whites directly:

> A trolley car comes along packed with 'fay people [white
> people] and a few colored people grabbing the trolley and the
> conductor to keep him from drivin' the trolley, while other
> people throw rocks and stones into the window causing seri-
> ous accidents. Half-juiced . . . the rest of the people grabs the
> trolley and begins lifting it into the air while the other people
> that was in the trolley climbs the window. . . . [T]he cops run
> over to the scene of the crime and start whippin' asses like
> hell, beats one colored man dam [*sic*] near to death before he
> let go the trolley.

Unlike race riots in the nineteenth or early twentieth centuries, in
which whites were the aggressors, the 1943 riot involved African-
American attacks on white-owned property and occasionally on white
commuters. It followed a year of clashes nationally, as African Americans and Euro-Americans fought nearly everywhere the color line was
crossed, especially on military bases and near defense plants where
African Americans were taking traditionally "white" jobs. In the
Harlem riot, young African-American males, like Claude Brown and R,
reveled in the carnivalesque reversal of the usual structures of power
and order and gave voice to a new rebellious spirit to which white
New Yorkers responded with predictable panic. R's warning, "I leave
this thought with thee, Do not attempt to fuck with me," could be
taken as an epigraph for a new era.

Race and Crime

One might expect that the disorders of 1943 would lead to a discovery of gangs, but they did not. There was no evidence of organized
gang participation in the riots, and when public officials encountered
reports of gang activity, they dismissed them as not serious. They
were caught up in what they viewed as a more important public
debate about increasing crime, which many white New Yorkers
blamed on African Americans. In the public furor over race and crime,
hints of the existence of street gangs were ignored.

The public debate over race and crime, initiated with reports of a
Harlem crime wave and continued after the Harlem riot, was now refu-
eled by the Brooklyn grand jury report of August 1943. Instead of
beginning a discussion of the problems of migration, displacement, and
poverty, the report sparked an attack on African-American migrants
[from the South]. Public authorities in turn, led by the liberal manor,
Fiorella La Guardia, defended the African-American community against

charges of criminality. This highly charged atmosphere contributed to officials downplaying reports of gang activity.

The Brooklyn grand jury complained that Bedford-Stuyvesant's "Little Harlem" existed in a state of lawlessness. They found that "many school children have been beaten, robbed and otherwise mistreated on dozens of occasions." Walking the streets after dark had become perilous, and "many fine churches have closed completely because their parishioners do not dare attend evening services." Citizens traveling on subways and buses had been assaulted, and groups of young boys, armed with knives and other weapons, "roam the streets at will and threaten and assault passersby and commit muggings and holdups with increasing frequency." Youths under twenty-one years of age were responsible for most crimes. "These children form into little groups, run into stores, steal merchandise and run away. They break windows; they snatch pocketbooks; they commit muggings, holdups, and assaults." Law-abiding citizens armed themselves in self-defense, thus reinforcing a cycle of violence. The grand jury blamed young, male, African-American migrants for the upsurge in crime. Moreover, as evidenced by the frequent references to problems with "groups," the Brooklyn grand jury was in the process of discovering gangs. . . .

Brooklyn citizens echoed the grand jury's charges about gangs. Louis Schachter, an attorney, wrote the mayor about gangs whose accomplishments included "beating of women, aged persons and children. Purse snatching and petty theft is a common occurrence. These boys . . . are known as The Saints, Falcons, The Bishops, The Beavers, and The 627 Stompers, among other names." Schachter concluded, "From my speaking to these people [residents], it appears to me that they are in mortal fear of the gangs in the area." Edwards Cleaveland, the chair of a committee for interracial relations, wrote, "We are much concerned over the activities of gangs of young boys and particularly so since the recent murder on Jefferson Ave. . . . The published accounts of this murder mention such gangs as the 'Robins' and the 'Bishops' whose members organize gang fights with knives and home made firearms." These were the fears not of rabid racists but of citizens—black and white, young and old—who saw themselves as potential victims of gang violence. Cleaveland wrote, "We have known of the existence of these gangs and of the terror which they inspire in young Negro boys who do not belong to them." Their voices were stilled, however, by the clamor over race and crime.

Public officials reacted skeptically to citizens' complaints about gangs. They rejected evidence of gangs, either by disparaging the credibility of witnesses or using the turn-of-the-century gang studies to reinterpret the meaning of what people were reporting. The police commissioner was among those who refused to acknowledge the existence of gangs in Bedford-Stuyvesant. Whatever offenses adolescents committed, they were, he argued, the acts of individuals and not of an "organized juvenile crime syndicate." The commissioner admitted that there were "groups of youths who associate together in this neighborhood, but such association is fundamentally no more expression of evil than the association of the members of a parish ball club." It was an expression of "natural instinct," a product of the "gang age." Police Commissioner Lewis Valentine borrowed the language and concepts of the early gang boy studies to dismiss residents' fear of gangs. Gangs were either the result of normal play activity or they belonged to the adult criminal world. No category existed in the gang boy studies for adolescent gangs whose playthings included firearms but who were not linked to organized crime. The Bishops and the Robins, according to Valentine, simply could not be.

The police who investigated the complaints of the citizens who wrote to the mayor were equally dismissive. In response to Louis Schachter's letter, police officials visited the local boys' club, where the gangs were alleged to congregate. The director told the police that "there are no gangs of boys known as the 'Saints, Falcons, Bishops, Beavers or the 627 Stompers.'" Police investigating Edwards Cleaveland's letter reported that accounts of the Bishops and Robins had been "greatly exaggerated. . . . They are not true gangs in that the organization is not tight and controlled, and leadership is not the task of any one member. Often these groups form because of athletic contests, assume bizarre names and titles, and then when the athletic season is over they will remain together chiefly because they are from the same locality or street." There was no evidence of anyone being terrorized; police only found the "overexuberance of misguided youth." . . . Officials continued to apply the concepts of the prewar gang studies to discredit citizens' reports of adolescent gang activity. Public officials could not see the gangs in front of them.

Gangs and Neighborhood Conflict

At the same time that public officials rejected reports about street gangs, evidence of their activity began to mount. As gang conflicts began to rage across ethnic lines, it became difficult to ignore them. Although police and political leaders denied the existence of gangs, New York citizens were discovering them. In neighborhoods where ethnic succession was occurring, existing Euro-American gangs took on the task of defending turf against the in-migration of Puerto Ricans and African Americans. Bradford Chambers, a journalist trained in sociology, was one of the first commentators to note the proliferation of gangs and the increasingly intense nature of gang conflict as different ethnic communities came into contact. Chambers argued that while gangs had a long history in New York, the inspiration for contemporary gang conflict lay in ethnic and religious hostility. Gangs were to be found in many city neighborhoods, but their activities were most charged in borderline districts, where "fear, suspicion and antag-onism" predominated. "The gangs in these communities have primar-ily one purpose—protective security." Here gangs were passing the "tipping point," as fear sparked gang formation and conflict followed.

Chambers investigated an area on the Upper West Side of Manhat-tan near City College that he called "Mousetown." African Americans and Puerto Ricans had breached the dividing line in west Harlem by crossing Amsterdam Avenue and moving west toward the Hudson, and the area's white youths were resisting. "When the traditional colored districts began to expand . . . the white boys' clubs, led by the Han-cocks, the Rainbows, and the Irish Dukes, turned to conflict. In adja-cent Harlem, the Negro Sabres, the Socialistics, and the Chancellors joined the battle." The key words here are "turned to conflict," as clubs or street-corner groups chose to become gangs and fight against African-American adolescents. This was a classic "defended neighbor-hood," in which corner groups patrolled the borders and watched passersby and, when faced with the "invasion" of another group, decided to resist. Some white adults, worried about the changing com-position of the area, encouraged gangs to attack African Americans. . . .

Gangs responded enthusiastically to adult support by throwing rocks through the apartment windows where African Americans lived, painting swastikas on the buildings, and hurling trash, debris, and paint-filled bottles into the lobbies of apartment buildings. Needless to say, wandering adolescents, both black and white, were subject to attack by different gangs solely on the basis of skin color. The *New York Times* reported that Frederick Teichmann, Jr., a fifteen-year-old pastor's son, was escorting two girls home from services in the Mouse-town area, when he was set upon and stabbed by an African-American gang that mistook him for a gang member. (Following what was reported as the "gang code," no attempt was made to rob Teichmann or to harm his companions.) Under such circumstances, many resi-dents, particularly those with children, saw their only choice as to flee. Boys from families unable or unwilling to leave joined gangs because, according to one boy quoted by Chambers in a 1948 article on gangs, "'it's just smarter for your health to belong, that's all.'"

Skirmishes of the variety found by Chambers were common in neighborhoods undergoing ethnic transition. All over New York, Euro-American adolescents forgot earlier rivalries and organized to defend neighborhood boundaries. For example, in the Tompkins Park neighborhood in Brooklyn, African Americans were moving into an area that had been largely Jewish, Italian, and Irish. White gangs had taken over an abandoned brewery, which was both a clubhouse and a fortress to which they retreated when threatened by others. A Brook-lyn community organization became alarmed enough to hire a street worker to investigate the situation. He found that "there were a num-ber of clicks [*sic*] that went to war, with the brewery and the street as battlegrounds. One fight was seldom enough. They fought for weeks at a stretch. When the police arrived the fighters had disappeared." The white gangs included the Brewery Rats, the Pulaski Street boys, the Clover Street boys, and the Red Skin Rhumbas, all of whom were bitter rivals. However, "whiteness" provided a common denominator around which the rivals could rally. When threatened by outsiders, the white gangs formed an uneasy alliance that lasted until the immediate threat disappeared. "During quieter intervals the larger group called together to engage in gang warfare splits up into several smaller groups [that] go by different names than does the whole group." This seemed to be a reflection of their essentially defensive posture. The street worker argued that they were "afraid of the colored groups immediately to the south and seem to exist in most part as a means of common defense against these gangs." White youths remained somewhat disorganized because they did not yet feel as pressured as did gangs in the Bronx and Harlem. Tompkins Park had still managed to avoid "real gang warfare."

"Real" gang warfare went beyond rumbles featuring chains, bats, car aerials, and rocks. Morrisania, in the South Bronx, was one of the neighborhoods where clashes were getting out of hand. Like other South Bronx neighborhoods, Morrisania had served as a refuge for Irish, Italian, and Jewish families fleeing the tenements of the Lower East Side or East Harlem. Now they felt under siege as Puerto Rican and African-American families followed in their footsteps. Father Banome, a Catholic priest at Saint Jerome's Church, reported, "'I was just amazed at the struggle between them [Irish and Puerto Ricans], the absolute hatred and disregard. It manifested itself mainly in gang fights.'" One such fight in the spring of 1945 between the Jackson Knights, a white gang, and the Slicksters, an African-American one, resulted in the death of thirteen-year-old Jesse Richardson. Members of the Slicksters had stolen a pair of eyeglasses from a member of the Knights, who plotted revenge. When a group of Slicksters approached the corner candy store that the Knights used as their headquarters, the Knights opened fire on them and killed Richardson. Police later confiscated two Springfield rifles, one Savage rifle, a bayonet, and two hundred rounds of ammunition. . . .

All over the city, but especially in neighborhoods undergoing ethnic succession, gangs were organizing, street-corner groups were transforming themselves into gangs, and adolescents were arming themselves and engaging in bitter skirmishes. . . . The gangs that public authorities could ignore in 1943 had become a major social problem they had to confront. It was clear by the end of the war that gangs were carving up neighborhoods into spheres of influence as readily as Roosevelt, Churchill, and Stalin had divided the world at Yalta. A war abroad had been replaced by a war at home, and public officials and the press were finally forced to acknowledge it.

THE ORIGINS OF MEXICAN AMERICAN GANGS

Rubén Martínez

Rubén Martínez is a journalist, performer, poet, and the author of *The Other Side: Notes from the New L.A., Mexico City, and Beyond.* In the following essay, Martínez explores the origins of Mexican American gangs from their early roots at the beginning of the twentieth century to the present day. The economic isolation of East Los Angeles barrios led to a breakdown in Mexican family tradition, he maintains, and the resulting lack of cultural identity forced Mexican American youths to form their own surrogate families—gangs.

The myth of the Outsider—the outlaw—is virtually as old as America, a cherished part of our folklore. In its early incarnations, it spoke to the country's sense of itself as a band of misfits on a quest for liberty. The pilgrims were religious or criminal outlaws. Depending on your perspective, early arrivals were Freedom Fighters or dangerous zealots, visionaries or evil incarnates. They were Americans.

Thus Billy the Kid—by all accounts a ruthless killer—still goes down in our cultural history as an American hero. The only prerequisite for such anointment is some sense that the outlaws had themselves been victims before they turned violent. Among the gunslingers of the Old West were Confederate soldiers who had faced devastation in the South. And in the 1920s and 1930s, Americans could project their frustrations over Prohibition and the Depression onto gangsters of the day. So while Bonnie and Clyde killed innocent bank clerks, they became heroine and hero to many in the soup lines who considered the crimes of big capital against working people at least as egregious as the gang's.

But today's street kids in the inner cities of America—Latino *"cholos"* and black *"gangstas"* (black and brown both use the term "homeboy," a noun sanctifying the only place they can call "home," their gang's own territory)—aren't heroes to anyone, perhaps not even to themselves. In fact, blacks and Mexicans never qualified for that status, even though they were authentic Outsiders in every way. Mexicans who turned to a life of crime in the Southwest after the Mexican-American War were never considered outlaws in the heroic sense. The gringos called them "bandidos," emphasizing ethnic otherness and conjuring an image of darkness and depravity. To Anglo Californians of the late 1800s, Joaquin Murietta—a legendary bandit-rebel—was a cold-blooded killer. But to Mexican-American Californians, he represented a virtual one-man insurrection against the gringos who had stolen their lands and dignity.

A few literary and cinematic portrayals in the late nineteenth and early twentieth centuries—the dashing "Spanish" romance of *Ramona*, The Cisco Kid, Zorro, etc.—did little to clean up the lingering bandido image. From the "greaser" character in *The Treasure of the Sierra Madre* who snarled at Humphrey Bogart about "steenking badges" to today's typical images of Chicanos as gangbangers, drug runners, lusty señoritas or matronly-types-with-many-babies, Hollywood carries 150-year-old cultural baggage in its representation of Mexican-Americans: Americans have never seen "Mexicans" as "Americans." They are always the Other, to be lusted after or feared.

The Evergreen gang of Los Angeles calls the Boyle Heights District home; it is part of greater East L.A., also known as the Eastside, one of the country's biggest and most mythologized barrios. East L.A. constantly vies with Spanish Harlem in the American pop imagination as stereotype of the Latin. Lowrider Chevrolets bouncing up and down on their hydraulic lifts. *Cholas* with foot-high bouffants and heavy mascara, Zoot Suiters with their outrageous "drapes," Mexican simpleton characters. These images are rooted in fragments of reality, of course, as are most stereotypes, but we laugh at these, as we do with many things we can't understand. The laughter is a product of the social distance between "us" and "them."

The Eastside Story

Prior to World War I, Boyle Heights and parts of unincorporated Los Angeles to the east of the city were relatively affluent areas; there are still a few elegant Victorians dotting the landscape. In the 1920s, cheaper housing and immigration made East L.A. a California version of New York's Lower East Side: Jews, Italians, Armenians, Japanese. East L.A.'s main commercial thoroughfare was even named "Brooklyn" in a nostalgic nod to the East Coast origins of many of the immigrants. (Recently the name was changed to "César Chávez," in honor of the late Chicano farmworker leader, but except for young Chicano radicals, most people still refer to it as "la Bru-kleen.")

At about the same time, the Mexican Revolution (1910–17) sent the first twentieth-century wave of Mexican immigrants to California. The early barrio was a ramshackle collection of houses and shacks in and around the historic center of the original Mexican pueblo at Olvera Street. (To this day, thousands of Mexicans and Chicanos are drawn by a race-memory magnet every Sunday to La Placita, the old pueblo church there.) Conditions ranged from livable to squalid, but, with the continuing flood of refugees, quickly grew unbearably dense, pushing those who were to become the pioneers of the Mexican barrio of East L.A. towards Boyle Heights.

From the beginning, the immigrant Mexicans were on their own in their new (though historically speaking old) home. Then as now, they did not come looking for welfare handouts—most first-generation Mexicans are too proud to even entertain the thought of any charity—but for work. There was plenty to be had. Agribusiness flourished throughout Los Angeles and Orange Counties; tens of thousands of Mexicans picked the orange groves of the San Fernando Valley. Brickyards, garment factories and, later, the automobile industry (General Motors, Firestone, Goodyear) were also stocked with Mexican labor.

Politically speaking, the Mexicans were on their own too, isolated from the Anglo power brokers at City Hall. And so they developed, like other groups of immigrants and refugees, *"mutualistas,"* mutual aid societies. Ties with Mexico remained strong. Revolutionaries like the Flores Magón brothers organized exile cadres in Los Angeles and other towns closer to the border for quixotic missions back home, did fundraising, promised a new Mexico for the refugees to return to.

But the new Mexico never really materialized, especially not in the impoverished lands of the northern and central provinces, where most of the refugees came from. And so what was to have been a temporary stay became permanent. The barrio continued to grow, and began its transformation into a "Mexican-American" community. By the 1940s, most of the European immigrants had moved on to the greener pastures of the booming San Fernando Valley and the Westside of Los Angeles. East L.A. came to be known as the "Mexican part of town," and was literally the other side of the tracks: the "height" in Boyle Heights is a gentle rise of land immediately east of the Santa Fe Railroad and the L.A. River.

Mexicans were not to go through the same rite of passage to Americanization as other immigrant groups: scapegoats for the Great Depression in California, they were sent back to Mexico by the hundreds of thousands in the Repatriation of the 1930s. And despite the fact that they were invited back to the picking fields and the factories for the war effort, and despite the fact that Mexican-Americans by the thousands signed up and were sent overseas (and won more medals proportionate to their number in the armed forces than any other group), at home they were still foreigners. Public swimming pools displayed signs announcing "Wednesdays for Mexicans Only." Schools were *de-facto* segregated. And the pachucos, the first urban Mexican-American gangs, quickly became the favorite whipping boys of local politicians and law enforcement.

The first pachuco cliques formed in East Los Angeles in the late

1920s and 1930s. By today's standards, they were innocent—fights were usually waged with fists, occasionally with knives and chains—and they resembled street toughs more than today's gangmembers. Aesthetics were all-important. The highstyle of the Zoot Suit (pants up near the breastbone, chain and fob swinging down below the knee) was an exaggeration, a subversion of typical American fashion. Like the lowrider cars of the sixties and seventies, the Zoot Suit wasn't meant to be worn so much as seen (although it had its functional side, too: loose clothes were perfect for the acrobatics of Chicano swing dancing, just as today's "baggies" allow for hip hop). It was a badge of cultural rebellion, and the virtual birth of Chicano culture: to Americans, the Zoot Suiters still looked Mexican; to Mexicans in the Old Country, they looked far too gringo.

The pachucos were seen as foreigners—despite the fact that their older brothers or dads and uncles were in the service—and easy targets for war-time xenophobia. The so-called Zoot Suit Riots of 1942 did not start, as the jingoistic *Los Angeles Times* of the era reported, with crazed Chicano youths attacking Anglo servicemen. Rather, off-duty sailors went on hunting expeditions, stripping and beating any "hoodlum" unlucky enough to be caught on the street wearing his "drapes."

The social walls around the barrio grew higher and higher. Consider historian Carey McWilliams's description of Chicano nightlife in 1940s Los Angeles:

> While the fancier 'palladiums' have known to refuse [the pachucos], even when they have had the price of admission, there are other dance halls, not nearly so fancy, that make a business of catering to their needs. It should be noted, however, that Mexican boys never willingly accepted these inferior accommodations and the inferior status they connote. Before they have visited the 'joints' on Skid Row, they have first tried to pass through palatial foyers on Sunset Boulevard. When they finally give up, they have few illusions left about their native land.

McWilliams, one of California's premier historians, served as chairman of the Sleepy Lagoon Defense Committee in the early 1940s, formed after an entire "gang" of Chicano youths was rounded up and convicted of murder in a trial that made a mockery of American jurisprudence—including an "expert" witness who testified that the Mexican "race" was predisposed to barbaric behavior because of its savage Indian ancestry (testimony that remained on the record). The enmity between law enforcement and Chicano youth thus dates back at least half a century.

This is heavily documented history. Two blue-ribbon panels (the McCone Commission which investigated the causes of the Watts Riots of 1965 and the Christopher Commission which looked into the

Rodney King incident in 1991) found that Mexicans or blacks participating in no obvious criminal activity are regularly taught a lesson by
the LAPD—whether they're hardcore gangmembers or innocent
party-crew types. Their cars are pulled over for purely harassment purposes. They are ordered to "assume the position," kneeling with
hands locked behind their heads.

The result is a severely limited world—a world hemmed in by fear.
Fear of the police, of "white" society, of the entire world beyond the
L.A. River. "I thought that Soto Street to Atlantic Boulevard to the
Sears building was the whole world," says Joey Pallares, a youth counselor at Wilson High School who grew up on the Eastside. "I thought
everyone was brown, that just teachers and doctors were white. I'd
never even been to the beach."

With the 1960s came heightened awareness of the barrio's social
and economic isolation. César Chávez and the United Farm Workers
marched and fasted, high school students across the Eastside staged
the famous "blowouts," walking out of classes to demand more
resources for barrio schools.

But the Chicano Movement itself highlighted old wounds over identity. Integrationists battled separatists: are we Mexican, or American, or
Mexican-American? From the time of the Mexican Revolution to the
passage in 1994 of Proposition 187 (which seeks to deny public education and health benefits to undocumented—*i.e.*, mostly Mexican-
immigrants), generation after generation of Mexican youth has faced
essentially the same quandary. Unlike the other immigrants—the Jews
and Poles, the Italians and Irish—who arrived at roughly the same
time, the Mexicans of the Eastside are still not considered Americans.
Proposition 187 recalls the Repatriation of the 1930s. The cops still
harass the kids. Barrio schools are still inferior. Chicanos are still
trapped between Old World ideals of family and solidarity and American notions of individual ambition and upward mobility.

Inner-city violence appears to have grown as the sense of isolation
and frustration deepens. Fistfights evolved into knife-fights, followed
by Old West-like gun duels, and, finally, drive-by shootings. There
are myriad explanations offered for the escalation: increased Mexican gang involvement in the drug trade; easier access to guns; the
failure of the civil rights movement (and liberal/ethnic politics) to
fundamentally transform inner-city life; the overall society's drift
toward a culture of violence. One cause stands out: the collapse in
the 1980s of Southern California's aerospace and automobile industries, once the primary source of upwardly mobile, union-scale jobs
for those in the barrio.

With nowhere to go, the barrio turns inward. The neighborhood
becomes the world, and families carry the weight of that world. The
Mexican culture's reliance on intimacy in the private realm (the
Catholic version of WASP "family values") appears to help set the

stage for both heroic and tragic events in the barrio. Fatherless house-holds, not uncommon even in Mexico, manage to survive with a sense of "us against the world," the world being the sheriff's depart-ment, rival gangmembers, bill collectors.

There are indications that even this most sacred of Mexican institu-tions is beginning to break apart. UCLA public health professor David Hayes-Bautista has noted that the healthiest barrio families are those that maintain their Mexican traditions—in diet, in child-rearing, in cultural rituals, etc. Children of first-generation immigrants are less prone to illness, injury, and death by violence than those of the sec-ond and third generation. In other words, Hayes-Bautista says, Ameri-can culture may be bad for the barrio's health.

As hope recedes, the barrio family continues to retreat into itself. It also works to repair itself: if the nuclear unit disintegrates, the extended family plays a crucial role: an aunt or uncle steps in if mother or father are gone; cousins can become surrogate siblings; grandparents often live with their children and their adult children's children. This notion of blood solidarity has probably saved more kids from the streets than all the "outreach" efforts combined, even before such programs were severely cut back in the late eighties.

At the same time, there are traits at the heart of the Mexican fam-ily that may be intimately related to gang violence. Do barrio moth-ers sometimes inadvertently reinforce their sons' violent behavior through a not-so-secret admiration of their exaggerated male bravado (a macho rebel onto which mothers can project their own frustra-tions)? Does the "intimacy" of the family become suffocating, as some sociologists have conjectured, and inhibit passage from adoles-cent rebellion to an adult sense of responsibility?

What is clear is that gangs proliferate in the barrio and in the 'hood as a response to public and private failure. The gang is the "family" of last resort: a family for kids when the parents are absent, abusive, or just worn down by the pressures of barrio life; a school when public education disintegrates; a culture unto itself when neither side of the U.S.-Mexican border seems to provide any sense of rootedness.

The vast majority of gang violence is internecine. The rage turns inward: the gang kid blows away his mirror image, another gang kid. Thus every drive-by shooting is nothing less than ethnic suicide, a bloodletting between brothers (and, increasingly, sisters). A good part of the war on the streets of the Eastside—with all its roots in politics, in economics, in a history of racism and self-negation—will likely be won or lost within the heart of the barrio family.

For countless gang and non-gang kids in the barrio, there is some-one . . . trying anything and everything to save them from the streets. The problem for the rest of us is that when we see the barrio—and we see it only through the media and Hollywood—we only see the vic-tims and perpetrators of the violence.

African American Street Gangs in California

California Department of Justice

The following excerpt from the California attorney general's 1993 report, *Gangs 2000: A Call to Action*, traces the history of African American street gangs in California, focusing primarily on the modern incarnations that are marked by crime, drug dealing, and violence. Emerging in the 1920s as loose neighborhood associations, African American gangs eventually began to build larger memberships in the late 1950s, primarily in the Compton and South Central neighborhoods of Los Angeles. The rival Crips and Bloods emerged in the late 1960s, setting the stage for decades of violent gang confrontation and crime. Starting in the 1980s, members of the Crips and Bloods spread across the United States, establishing networks of their gangs in other cities.

African American gangs began forming in California during the 1920s. They were not territorial; rather, they were loose associations, unorganized, and rarely violent. They did not identify with graffiti, monikers, or other gang characteristics.

These early gangs consisted generally of family members and neighborhood friends who involved themselves in limited criminal activities designed to perpetrate a "tough guy" image and to provide an easy means of obtaining money.

From 1955 to 1965, the African American gangs increased with larger memberships and operated primarily in south central Los Angeles and Compton. This was partly due to more African American youths bonding together for protection from rival gangs.

The Rise of the Crips and the Bloods

It was not until the late 1960s when the Crips and Bloods—the two most violent and criminally active African American gangs—originated. The Crips began forming in southeast Los Angeles by terrorizing local neighborhoods and schools with assaults and strong-arm robberies. They developed a reputation for being the most fierce and feared gang in the Los Angeles area.

Excerpted from *Gangs 2000: A Call to Action*, by the California Department of Justice, March 1993.

Other African American gangs formed at about the same time to protect themselves from the Crips. One such gang was the Bloods, which originated in and around the Piru Street area in Compton, California; thus, some Bloods gangs are referred to as Piru gangs. The Bloods, which were outnumbered at the time by the Crips three to one, became the second most vicious African American gang in the Los Angeles area.

Both the Crips and Bloods eventually divided into numerous smaller gangs (or "sets") during the 1970s. They kept the Crips and Bloods (Piru) name, spread throughout Los Angeles County, and began to claim certain neighborhoods as their territory. Their gang rivalry became vicious and bloody.

By 1980, there were approximately 15,000 Crips and Bloods gang members in and around the Los Angeles area. The gangs—or sets—ranged in size from a few gang members to several hundred and had little, if any, organized leadership. The typical age of a gang member varied from 14 to 24 years old.

Initiation into a gang required the prospective member to "jump in" and fight some of the members already in the gang. Another initiation rite required them to commit a crime within the neighborhood or an assault against rival gang members.

They remained territorial and motivated to protect their neighborhoods from rival gang members. They established unique and basic trademarks such as colors, monikers, graffiti, and hand signs. The color blue was adopted by the Crips as a symbol of gang recognition; red became the color of the Bloods. Monikers—such as "Killer Dog," "12-Gauge," and "Cop Killer"—often reflected their criminal abilities or their ferociousness as gang members. Graffiti identified the gang and hand signs displayed symbols—usually letters—unique to the name of their gang. It was not unusual for members to "flash" hand signs at rival gang members as a challenge to fight. They took great pride in displaying their colors and defending them against rival gangs. They were willing to die for the gang, especially in defense of their colors and neighborhood. It was not until the early 1980s that the era of drive-by shootings began.

The gangs became involved in a variety of neighborhood crimes such as burglary, robbery, assault, and the selling of marijuana, LSD, and PCP. The issue of gang involvement in narcotics trafficking was generally considered to be of a minor nature prior to the 1980s. However, by 1983, African American Los Angeles gangs seized upon the availability of narcotics, particularly crack, as a means of income. Crack had supplemented cocaine as the most popular illicit drug of choice. Prime reasons for the widespread use of crack were its ease of conversion for smoking, the rapid onset of its effect on the user, and its comparatively inexpensive price.

The migration of African American Los Angeles gang members during the 1980s to other United States cities, often for reasons other than some vast gang-inspired conspiracy, resulted in the spread of crack sales and an attendant wave of violence. This spread of crack sales can be traced back to the gang members' family ties in these cities and to the lure of quick profits. These two reasons provided most of the inspiration and motivation for the transplanted gang members.

Considerable diversity is displayed by Crips and Bloods gangs and their members in narcotics trafficking, which allows for different levels of involvement from narcotic selling by adolescents to the more important roles of directing narcotics trafficking activities. In the past, an individual's age, physical structure, and arrest record were often principal factors in determining gang hierarchy; money derived from narcotic sales soon became the symbol which signified power and status.

Crips and Bloods have established criminal networks throughout the country and capitalized on the enormous profits earned from the trafficking and selling of crack cocaine. In 1987, nine members of the Nine-Deuce Hoovers—a Crips gang—migrated from Los Angeles to Seattle, Washington, where they ran three crack houses, with crack transported from California each week. One gang member was subsequently arrested and pleaded guilty in 1988 to selling crack near a school and using a gun to further his narcotic enterprise. He was sentenced to 25 years in prison and is currently incarcerated in Leavenworth Federal Prison, Kansas.

Trends and Patterns in the 1990s

The Department of Justice estimates there could be as many as 65,000 African American gang members in California today. The majority of them are still Crips and Bloods gang members. They now range in age from 12 to 35, with some as old as 40. The gangs vary in size from 30 members to as many as 1,000. They continue to fight each other for narcotic-related profits and in defense of territory, and many remain unstructured and informal. A few of them are becoming organized with some definitive gang structure.

Some of the older gang members—known as "Original Gangsters"—who have been in the gang for a long time are often the recruiters and trainers of new gang members. Many are second- and third-generation gang members and have been incarcerated in the California Youth Authority or the California Department of Corrections. Due to their propensity for violence, prison and jail officials have found it necessary to house hardcore members in high-security cell blocks or separate facilities.

Some of the more experienced gang members are beginning to abandon established characteristics, such as wearing the colors blue and red, and are now trying to disguise their gang affiliation by wearing nondescript black and white clothing. Other members continue to rely on the gang trademarks, and neighborhoods abound with graffiti signifying the presence of Crips and/or Bloods gangs.

Some of the gangs have formed alliances with other ethnic gangs, and some Crips and Bloods gangs include Hispanic or Asian gang members. Female gang members are rare, but those who do participate play a minor role in gang activity and are used to rent crack houses or traffic in narcotics.

The Drug Trade

The Crips and Bloods continue to control the distribution of crack cocaine in several California cities and other states. Federal and state law enforcement authorities report Crips and Bloods gang members in 33 states and 123 cities. Once they arrive in a city, they determine the demand for narcotics, the identity of major narcotic dealers, and the existence of established narcotic operations. They then recruit new gang members and take over the selling of crack cocaine. Sometimes, the takeover is without violence if there is little or no resistance from rival gangs. Other times, there will be a great deal of violence if existing gangs have already established narcotic operations, which compete for the narcotics trade. . . .

With gang involvement in the crack market comes a tremendous increase of street-level violence as they battle over the profitable narcotics trade. Violence is a routine part of doing business, and it is used to terrorize citizens and other gangs resisting their intrusion. They make no effort to distinguish between intended rival gang victims or innocent bystanders.

Besides crack cocaine, African American gang members also sell marijuana and PCP, and some have purchased chemicals for their own production of PCP.

Their use of weapons has evolved to high-powered, large-caliber handguns and automatic and semi-automatic weapons including AK-47 assault rifles and Mac-10s with multiple-round magazines, and they sometimes wear police-type body armor. Gang attacks on police officers have escalated. Gangs—such as the '89 Gangster Crips, Project Crips, Neighborhood Crips, Southside Compton Crips, and the Pueblo Bishop Bloods—have shot at officers during vehicle pursuits, narcotic investigations, robberies, and responses to family disturbances.

Their other crimes range from robberies, burglaries, grand thefts, receiving stolen property, and witness intimidations to assaults with a deadly weapon, drive-by shootings, and murders. In Los Angeles during 1990, there were 135 homicides, 1,416 assaults and batteries, and 775 robberies attributed to Crips and Bloods gang members.

Some specific targets of criminal activities include jewelry stores. A series of armed robberies, which have been connected to Crips gang members from the Los Angeles area, have occurred in several Central Valley and San Francisco Bay Area cities. These armed robberies target jewelry stores and are committed by the "One-Minute Gang"—based on their ability to complete the robberies in one minute. Many robberies have occurred in California, and similar robberies are being reported in Nevada, Oregon, and Georgia. Some of the robberies have resulted in the theft of $150,000 to $250,000 worth of jewelry. An estimated combined loss of $4.7 million has been reported.

Another area of emerging criminal activities for the Crips and Bloods is theft of personal computers from stores and warehouses. In 1991, there were 19 such thefts in the Los Angeles and Orange County areas attributable to these gangs.

Gang Violence During the L.A. Riots

During the April 29 to May 1, 1992, riot in Los Angeles, some of the violence was attributed to the Crips and Bloods. The riot was the worst civil disorder in modern American history. Sixty persons died, some 2,500 were injured, 750 fires were set, 14,000 people were arrested, and upwards of $700 million in damage was done.

Gang members were involved in assaults, attempted murders, murders, arson, and looting. During the riot, two members of the 8-Trey Gangster Crips and two other individuals were seen on national television beating and robbing a truck driver. Twenty-two members of another Crips gang were arrested for looting approximately $80,000 worth of merchandise from electronic stores.

Other Crips and Bloods gang members were responsible for looting many of the 4,500 weapons from gun dealers, sporting goods stores, and pawn shops during the riot. Gang members indicated they would use the weapons to kill police officers and parole and probation officers via drive-by shootings and ambushes. Gang members graffitied walls with "187 L.A.P.D." (187 is the California Penal Code Section for homicide), and other gang members circulated flyers stating, "Open Season on LAPD."

A temporary truce between some of the gang members of the Crips and Bloods occurred in the Los Angeles area following the riot. Many of these gang members wore articles of red and blue clothing interweaved to show their unity. These gangs claimed the truce would unite their forces to target law enforcement officers; however, there have been no attacks against the officers resulting from this gang alliance.

CHAPTER 2

THE EXPANDING
IDENTITY OF GANGS

THE WIDE VARIETY OF GANGS

The Gang Crime Prevention Center

Located in Chicago, The Gang Crime Prevention Center works to develop long-term and practical solutions to the growing problem of street gangs. According to the following article by the center, it is difficult to precisely categorize street gangs because no two are identical. They vary in size, structure, and activities from community to community. Some are tightly knit, while others are loosely organized. Street gangs engage in all manner of activities, from the criminal to the mundane. Because of their unsteady social nature, gangs also experience a tremendous turnover in members and leaders, which can lead to ambiguity about the nature of a particular gang. However, the center concludes, most street gangs do share some common elements despite their diversity.

There are many different types of gangs. Street gangs are one type (as opposed to outlaw biker gangs, for example), but there are many variations of the "street gang." Because the street gang varies so much across place and time, it is hard to define—and therefore identify—precisely and accurately.

How Street Gangs Vary

Street gangs are diverse in terms of size, structure, membership composition, and activities. Along these dimensions they tend to vary from one community to the next, and even within the same community. No two street gangs are identical. Plus, nearly every street gang has multiple sub-groups, or small clusters of similarly aged gang members who come together around common interests and issues. Owing to tremendous internal differentiation, even a single street gang cannot be described accurately as uniform. So, gangs vary in relation to one another across and within communities, and the individual street gang varies within itself. All of this variation in group properties makes the street gang hard to define, measure, and respond to.

Street gangs exhibit varying degrees of structure, organization, and cohesion. They aren't all tightly knit or highly structured by any means. Some are very cohesive criminal enterprises with clear and strong leadership at the top, while most are loose confederations of youth and adults whose associations grow out of the shared troubles of their respective biographies. Some gangs have the characteristics of formal organizations, such as charters, by-laws, constitutions, and rituals for initiation and "graduation." Most gangs have few of these organizational attributes; they are instead collections of weakly bonded young people who operate according to casual, informal, and largely unspoken/unwritten rules.

Street gangs are hard to define for other reasons, too. As porous social groups, gangs experience tremendous turnover of members. Youth come and go, often staying involved for about a year before moving on. New "vacancies" usually get filled quickly. Gang leadership also changes over time. A leader today may be gone tomorrow because of a family move, voluntary disaffiliation, or incarceration. Another challenge to defining the street gang is the ambiguity surrounding gang membership. That the group itself defies precise definition makes it equally difficult to define and identify the gang member. Knowing who's in a gang and who isn't requires knowing what the gang is—otherwise, it's anybody's guess as to whether a given youth or adult can be classified as a gang member. The constant flux of the typical gang's membership and leadership make the street gang hard to define.

Street gang members engage in a wide range of activities, from the legal to the illegal, the mundane to the extraordinary. Although street gangs orient themselves to the breaking of laws and social norms, they also spend a lot (if not most) of their time just hanging out, wasting time, doing nothing much at all. Life in the street gang most commonly involves hours and hours of boredom and languor. Besides wasting time and foreclosing on future opportunities to become productive members of civil society, most street gang members do what most of their non-gang peers do—go to work, go to parties, participate in recreation and mating rituals, and engage in minor offending. When street gang members offend, they do so with great variation and with greater frequency than their non-gang counterparts. Very few gangs, taken as a whole, specialize in a particular kind of criminal or delinquent offending. Some individual members have expertise doing a certain kind of offense, such as motor vehicle theft. But in the aggregate, street gang members engage in "cafeteria style" offending, meaning they do a little bit of everything in terms of their crime and delinquency.

Conflicting Agendas

Further complicating the task of defining gangs is the fact that so many people and organizations are charged with defining gangs, each with its own unique agenda. An organization's definition of gang usually says more about the organization's mission or agenda than it does about the reality of the problem it's claiming to define and remedy. For example, a school administrator might be fearful that high numbers of gang incidents in and around schools would reflect poorly on the school and/or cause an overreaction by the community or the local police agency. She or he might therefore take a conservative approach to the problem by narrowly defining the term "gang incident," the hope being to preserve the school's reputation, forestall community outcry, and keep the police agency at bay. This entire strategy, while depressing the number of gang incidents in the school's records, may well be geared toward allowing the school enough time to address the problem in its own way.

The local police agency's executive officials, who command the overlapping jurisdiction, may use a broader definition in the belief that their charge is to ensure public safety through intensive policing. In this particular example the police agency's leadership might choose to define the street gang much more broadly than does the school, because a broader definition allows for more sweeping, larger-scale police intervention. In addition, this agency might be applying for grant funds to support "gang suppression," and the greater the number of gang incidents, the greater the likelihood of winning the grant.

This simplified example illustrates some of the difficulties that local agencies encounter when they attempt to define the gang problem by drawing more on their organizational mandate than on the nature of the problem in the community. Clearly, the school and the police agency share a serious concern over the same population and its activities. How they define the population and respond to what its members do will very likely differ in style, content, and outcome. At the very least, the two agencies will isolate themselves from each other, working independently to solve the problem, even when doing so means compromising the community's overall dedication to improving the quality of life for all citizens.

In the critical struggle to gain a deeper understanding of gangs and gang members, the term "street gang" often is more of a hindrance than a help. Individually and taken as a whole, the hundreds of different definitions of the term mask more than they reveal about the reasons behind the involvement of gang members in crime and delinquency. More often than not, the term actually inhibits the development of an accurate understanding of what gangs do and why they are a problem. Besides its vagueness, the term—with its infinite number of definitions—tends to evoke strong emotional responses, ranging from angry denial to myopic overreaction.

So What Is a Gang?

Street gangs are symptomatic of underlying problems in the lives of individual youth and in the life of the community. These problems are typically economic, social, and/or psychological in nature. Just as there is no single condition that causes a youth to join a gang or a gang to emerge in a particular neighborhood, there is no single remedy. The term "gang" is shorthand; the gang itself isn't the problem. Instead, the gang signifies multiple, overlapping problems that accumulate over time in the individual lives of its members and in the social life of the group whose initiates convene through common interests, shared troubles, and a unifying alternative culture.

Generally speaking, most street gangs—despite their diversity—have some common elements. Most are composed of youth and young adults who act together in committing criminal and delinquent offenses. Street gangs tend to be self-determining—that is, they are not sponsored by or supported by legitimate, law-abiding "parent" organizations. The typical street gang recognizes itself as a street gang, and residents of the surrounding neighborhood also recognize the gang as such. Ordinarily, the street gang claims and vigilantly defends a particular territory, or turf, such as a street corner or portion of a city block (although "traveling" gangs appear to be increasingly common). Each street gang customarily has a unique system of communication, a shared culture that guides members' actions and aids them in interpreting the actions of each other and of outsiders. Gang members orient themselves—their thoughts, beliefs, values, and actions—to crime and delinquency. Breaking the law is integral to the life of a typical street gang member.

Given all the diversity of street gangs, and the widespread disagreement over what they are, the greatest challenge for any neighborhood is to know its gangs well. Not knowing about the gang one encounters means not having one of the most useful tools for reducing the gang's negative effects on public life: an accurate understanding of the gang. Accumulating a solid knowledge base is a crucial first step in the long and perhaps unending process of treating the street gang's underlying causal conditions.

Uncertain Numbers

How many gangs, or gang members are there in Illinois? There is no way of knowing for sure. The answer to this question depends on (1) how "gang" is defined, and (2) who's doing the counting. Because there is no single, universally accepted definition, there is no single, universally accepted reliable estimate. Mainstream service organizations (public and private) are generally thought to be the source of such estimates. And as we have already discussed, the typical organization defines and counts gangs to further its own mission, thereby neglecting in many instances the true nature of the problem. Social service agencies define and count for the purpose of remedial intervention. Police agencies define and count for the purpose of deterring gang crime. Definitions utilized by social service agencies tend to be different than those utilized by police agencies. Moreover, definitions from police agency to police agency and from social service agency to social service agency vary according to many factors. Further compounding the problem of counting according to a given definition is the widespread practice of a single agency having more than one definition of gang, each with its own purpose.

In any event, there are more important things to know about gangs and gang members than how many there are. Answering the question "How many?" is a dead end street—it leads to little else but a number, which means nothing in the absence of more precise knowledge of how and why the number was calculated. What gang members actually do with their time is of much greater concern; an accurate and detailed understanding of their activities—legal and illegal, pro-social and deviant—will stand a much greater chance of leading to sensible policies and programs for reducing the destructive effects of street gangs on their communities. . . .

Crime and Delinquency

Why are gangs a problem? Because they facilitate crime and delinquency. Gang members are responsible for a disproportionate share of criminal and delinquent offenses. In other words, they are responsible for more than their fair share of offenses given their population's size relative to the total number of non-gang offenders. When in a gang, youth and adults are more delinquent/criminal than their non-gang delinquent/criminal counterparts. Being in a gang increases (1) the gang member's rate of offending, and (2) the seriousness of the offenses committed by the gang member. Gangs facilitate the crime and delinquency of their members because as deviant social groups they offer:

- positive reinforcements for anti-social and illegal norms, values, beliefs, attitudes, and behaviors
- a place where anti-social, delinquent, and criminal offenders can learn new, and improve existing, techniques for offending and for evading detection
- the often illusory promise of excitement, riches, adventure, protection, or nurturance (love, affection, and a sense of belonging), the unlikely attainment of which frequently involves criminal and delinquent offending

From one community to the next, street gangs emerge and/or proliferate for many different reasons. Within a single community the causes of street gang formation and proliferation also vary, across both space and time as well as socio-cultural milieu. Hence, the greatest obstacle to understanding the "street gang problem" is that the term denotes many things. No single construct can universally explain what particular communities are facing with respect to the delinquency and crime occurring in the context of deviant groups. In short, there is no "single gang problem." Instead, there are dozens of variations, typically sharing some common themes.

Where are gangs a problem? Gang problems occur most prevalently in larger cities; however, many smaller communities do experience gang activity, though often to a lesser degree. Still, though, rural and suburban communities are more likely than ever to be facing street gang problems. Most suburban and rural street gangs are homegrown; that is, their origins are indigenous to the community in that local youth and young adults begin to congregate on the basis of shared experiences, world view, and life interests. Extremely rare are the cases of major urban gangs dispatching hard core members to non-gang communities for the purpose of setting up a "franchise" or "satellite" gang. While these corporate moves do occur sporadically, they do not represent the norm. Whether homegrown or transplanted, the American street gang poses a threat to every community.

THE RISE OF GIRL GANGS

Catherine Edwards

In the following article, Catherine Edwards examines the growing popularity of gangs among young women. While girl gang
members once merely served as "cheerleaders" for their gangster
boyfriends, she explains, in recent years they have become a
force to be reckoned with in their own right. No longer content
to be auxiliary members of boy gangs, Edwards notes, girls are
frequently forming their own gangs, which are often as violent
and as sophisticated in crime as their male counterparts. Edwards
is a staff writer for *Insight on the News*, a weekly news magazine.

Shermika Booker is a different person today than she was two years
ago. She smiles, talks about how glad she is that she finished high
school and says she hopes someday to become a dental assistant. But
things were not so rosy in 1998.

Booker, 20, and a group of other girls who also live in the Garfield
neighborhood in upper Northwest Washington, D.C.—just two miles
from the White House—had a "beef," or fight, with the girls of a
nearby housing development called Park Moreton. The Garfield girls
dubbed themselves the "Shank 'Em Up Honeys"; their enemies at
Park Moreton were the "No Limit Honeys." Rivalry escalated to violence and the girls fought with knives, or shanks, and guns.

Female Gang Membership Is on the Rise

Teen-age girls trying to kill each other? None who watched the rival
Sharks and Jets meet for a "rumble" in *West Side Story* would recognize gangs today. These days, authorities are learning to keep their
eyes open for middle-school girls and their high-school mentors
who play as rough—or rougher—as the boys. "It's like gender libera-
tion has hit the gangs," John Anderson, deputy district attorney for
Orange County, Calif., told the Orange County Register in the early
1990s. "Girl gangsters aren't going to knock you down; they're
going to make you hurt and make it last." And that was then.
Female gang membership has continued to increase as lawmakers,
law-enforcement officials and community groups scramble to resist
this bizarre phenomenon.

In 1991 a group of eight men, all friends and native Washingtoni-ans, met in the hair salon of Tyrone Parker, now president of the Alliance of Concerned Men, an organization that brokered the truce that eventually ended the fighting between rival toughs. Concerned that the neighborhoods of the nation's capital had become much more dangerous than when they grew up, they decided to start meeting with the most violent kids in the city. Nine years later, the men have helped establish positive programs for young people all over Washington.

When fighting broke out among individual girls in the rival neighborhoods of Northwest Washington, their parents—for what-ever reason—were not involved in the lives of their kids, and many of the girls organized for protection, says Mack Alsobrooks of the Alliance. "They started dropping out of school and arming themselves. Some of the girls became prisoners in their own homes," he explains.

"If it wasn't for the Alliance, I'd still be on the streets," Booker states. But most teen-age girls who become involved in neighborhood violence and gang warfare are not so lucky. "We are predisposed to male gang members with our mentoring programs. Everything we do for males we now need to do for females," says Det. Sgt. Scott Lawson of the Polk County Sheriff's Department in Florida. He helped start the gang unit in the Lakeland region in 1995. "They are no longer second-class gangs. We cannot ignore them. They are selling drugs and doing drive-by shootings."

Lawson tells of his surprise at investigating a crime spree by a group in his county called the Gangster Disciples. The 10 gang mem-bers had committed armed robbery, assault, burglary and a shooting. "While this may seem run-of-the mill gang crime, what got our attention was that eight of the 10 members were females and a female was calling the shots for this particular outing," he says.

The numbers of incarcerated women have tripled since the late 1980s, according to the FBI's Uniform Crime Reports. While violent-crime rates are decreasing nationally, female juvenile crime is on the increase. Total crime arrests of female juveniles increased 118 percent between 1987 and 1996. In 1989, eight males were arrested for every female. At the close of the 1990s, that ratio was down to 5-to-1. The percentage of female gang involvement nationally is estimated at 10 to 15 percent; their ages range from 9 to 24.

Sophisticated and Dangerous

"They are not doing typical female crimes anymore either, like pros-titution," says Sandra Hahn of the Washington County, Minn., Department of Court Services. "They are committing violent as well as white-collar crime, computer-chip theft, phone cloning, ATM cash-card cloning. They are smart. Because they might not be as strong as males they use weapons like knives and razor blades and go for the face in a fight."

Hahn says she is concerned whether officers are properly trained in handling girl gangsters, and she travels nationally to train and educate authorities about how to deal with female offenders. She started monitoring girls in gangs through "ride-alongs" into gang territory with the Los Angeles Police Department when California was almost alone in tracking female gang involvement. She found that there was not a great deal of information on girls in gangs and that many in law enforcement as recently as the mid-1990s never had considered that females could be as violent—let alone more dangerous—than males.

"The girls used to be the cheerleaders for their gang-member boyfriends and actually served as deterrents for crimes because the boys wanted to protect them," notes Mike Knox, formerly with the Houston Police Department and author of *Gangsta in the House*. "The big trend now is for girls to form their own gangs, and some are in competition with the male gangs. Young women are realizing they can engage in all manner of crime like men."

Characteristics of Girl Gangsters

The Chicago Crime Commission, a nonprofit organization dedicated to improving public safety in the greater Chicago area, issued a study on girls in gangs in 1999. It found that girl gangsters tended to fall into four categories: auxiliary members of male gangs, female members of co-ed gangs, female leaders within co-ed gangs and all-female gangs. The female members wear the gang colors with as much pride as their male counterparts. They even feminize their gang names. Instead of Latin Kings, they call themselves the Latin Queens. They are not just Gangster Disciples but Lady Disciplettes. Girls are organized in white-supremacist gangs, Asian gangs, Pakistani gangs, African-American gangs and Latino and Latina gangs.

According to George Knox, editor of the *Journal of Gang Research* at the National Gang Crime Research Center in Chicago, initiation for female gang members is as harsh as for the males. Girls either go through a "jump in," which may require a violent beating from gang members, or a "sex in." But girls who are initiated into the gang by a "sex in" usually do not command the same respect as those "jumped in" and are less likely to rise in the ranks, says Knox. He notes how shocked the public was about a case in Texas in which two teen-age girls were required to have sex with HIV-positive gang members as part of the initiation ceremony.

Many male gang members sport elaborate tattoos denoting their affiliation. The girls also are tattooed. Detectives say that if girls are part of a male gang, they often are asked to commit crimes at the gang leader's bidding. In addition, many law-enforcement officers interviewed for this article conceded that girls are able to get away with more criminal activity. "Cops are less suspicious of a girl driving by with a baby in the back seat," says Mike Knox.

Some females are lured into gangs by the promise of financial reward, identity and status, according to Kristen Lindberg, author of the Chicago Crime Commission report on girl gangsters. Lindberg also notes that females are more likely to hold down a respectable job at the same time that they are involved in gang activity, also making them look less suspicious. Some of the police officers with whom Lindberg spoke said they seldom question the girls at crime scenes.

Females seem to put up with a great deal of mistreatment by their gang leaders. "I found that many of the girls had come from extremely exploitive and abusive backgrounds," says Hahn. "When the gang leaders treated them poorly, they thought this was normal behavior." Teen-age mothers often join gangs to provide a surrogate family for their children. "We now have 25-year-old grandmothers in gangs," reports Mike Knox. Other girl gangsters don't want to be subject to the authority of the boys. They join girl gangs because they have become tired of being the ones committing the crimes, running the drugs and putting themselves in danger, says Hahn.

Vietnamese Girl Gangs

Others from more traditional ethnic backgrounds want to form their own gangs to break out of inherited second-class-citizen roles that their mothers play. "Things that happen around the world affect us here in law enforcement," explains Bruce Wiley, a detective with the gang unit in Fairfax County, Va. "When Vietnam fell, refugees flooded to the U.S.; the same with the strife in El Salvador. A small number of these immigrants began taking advantage of the system and forming gangs."

Westminster, Calif., a town of 80,000 that lies 40 miles west of Los Angeles, has the largest Vietnamese business district in the free world. Sgt. Marcus Franks, a detective and gang investigator with the organized-crime unit there, says, "This is the center of Vietnamese gangs in the United States." His team has counted seven all-female Southeast Asian gangs in the area.

The first Vietnamese girl gangsters had come straight from the refugee camps, says Franks, so life in the United States was frightening but liberating. Teaming up with their male friends in gangs provided financial and social security that these girls never had experienced. But more than 25 years have passed since the end of the Vietnam War, and the first generation of American-born Vietnamese is doing its own thing. "They never had the refugee-camp experience," says Franks. "They see Occidental gangs in the media and want to pattern themselves after them. They are seriously engaged in organized crime, and some aspire to be an Asian John Gotti."

Franks notes that the girls have incredibly low self-esteem because they have rejected their ethnic culture but are not fully embraced by the male gangs because they are in competition with them. "This makes them work to be more tough and ultimately as dangerous," he says.

Wiley monitors Vietnamese gangs in Northern Virginia and recently worked a case in which a group of girl gangsters beat a 14-year-old girl within an inch of her life. "She said the wrong thing about a rival gang and they made her pay for it," he states.

Dealing with the Problem

Denial is the biggest problem among parents, educators, law enforcement, community and church groups, says Wiley. "No one wants to admit that their little girl could be involved in a gang. I spend a great deal of time going around talking about gang problems and educating people and police academies about what to look for. Parents must be involved in their kids' lives if we are going to curb gang growth," he says.

There is no law against being in a gang. Most are efficiently run and leaders command absolute authority. One of the most well-known gang leaders is Larry Hoover. He runs the Gangster Disciples from prison in Illinois, where he is serving a sentence of 200 years. The gang even has a Website. Gang members tend to thrive in prison, where gangs are very powerful, says Mike Knox.

Many juvenile offenders are sent to "boot camp," a punishment meant to reform wayward youth. Boot camps have been a topic of controversy as lawmakers debate their effectiveness in fighting crime. "We are training our juvenile gang members by sending them to boot camp," Wiley complains. "They come out tougher and stronger, ready more than ever for gang warfare."

"Kids don't need boot-camp foolishness, and they can be controlled without gun control and TV control. You've got to control their hearts," insists Robert Woodson, president of the National Center for Neighborhood Enterprise, a Washington-based organization dedicated to assisting low-income, self-help groups nationwide. Woodson acknowledges that girl gangs often go unnoticed and are a growing problem in many communities. He advocates intervention on a local level and supports the work of the Alliance of Concerned Men.

Alsobrooks of the Alliance of Concerned Men says that the warring Washington neighborhoods of Garfield and Park Moreton have been violence-free for two years because the girls realized that the enemies they were stabbing and shooting were a lot like themselves. He acknowledges that girls, in particular, need encouragement and self-esteem. "We give out a lot of hugs," he says.

"We are all friends now," Booker states. Alsobrooks smiles, and says, "Yes, our ladies are magnificent."

PRISON GANGS

Tiffany Danitz

In the following article, Tiffany Danitz reports on the proliferation of gang activity inside the walls of prisons since the early
1990s. She explains that some of these gangs originate inside
prisons, while in other cases, incarcerated members of street
gangs band together during their time in jail. According to investigators, Danitz writes, leaders of prison gangs are often able to
control the activities of their gang brethren on the outside. She
also describes the difficulties faced by law enforcement in combating these highly organized and secretive gangs. Danitz is an
education reporter for the online magazine Stateline.org and a
former staff writer for *Insight on the News*.

Prison gangs are flourishing across the country. Organized, stealthy
and deadly, they are reaching out from their cells to organize and
control crime in America's streets.

A 40-year-old gang leader uses his cellular phone to organize an
elaborate drug ring and order hits. He commands respect. He wears
gang-banger clothing and drapes himself with gold chains. This man
is responsible for an entire network of gang members across the state
of Illinois. He is Gino Colon, the mastermind behind the Latin Kings.
When prosecutors finally caught up with him in August 1998, Colon
was indicted for running the Latin Kings' drug-dealing operation from
behind prison walls—the state penitentiary in Menard.

"People in society and correctional officers need to understand that
immediate control over the prison system is often an illusion at any
time," says Cory Godwin, president of the gang-investigators association for the Florida Department of Corrections, or DC. "Contraband
equals power."

Prison gangs are flourishing from California to Massachusetts. In
1996, the Federal Bureau of Prisons found that prison disturbances
soared by about 400 percent in the early nineties, which authorities
say indicated that gangs were becoming more active. In states such as
Illinois, as much as 60 percent of the prison population belong to
gangs, Godwin says. The Florida DC has identified 240 street gangs
operating in their prisons. Street gangs, as opposed to gangs originat-

ing in prisons, are emerging as a larger problem on the East Coast.

Of the 143,000 inmates Texas houses in state pens, 5,000 have been identified as gang members and another 10,000 are under suspicion. Texas prison-gang expert Sammy Buentello says the state's prisons are not infested with gangs, but those that have set up shop are highly organized. "They have a paramilitary type structure," he says. "A majority of the people that come in have had experience with street-gang membership and have been brought up in that environment accepting it as the norm. But some join for survival."

Outside Influence

After James Byrd Jr. was dragged to death in Jasper, Texas, in June 1998, rumors spread throughout Texas linking two of the suspected assailants to racially charged prison gangs. While authorities and inmates dismiss these rumors, the Jasper murder occurred only weeks after a San Antonio grand jury indicted 16 members of the Mexican Mafia, one of the state's largest and most lethal prison gangs, for ordering the deaths of five people in San Antonio from within prison walls.

"As they are being released into the community on parole, these people are becoming involved in actions related to prison-gang business. Consequently, it is no longer just a corrections problem—it is also a community problem," Buentello states.

According to gang investigators, the gang leaders communicate orders through letters. Where mail is monitored they may use a code—for instance, making every 12th word of a seemingly benign letter significant. They use visits, they put messages into their artwork and in some states they use the telephone. "It is a misnomer that when you lock a gang member up they fall off to Calcutta. They continue their activity," Godwin emphasizes. "It has only been in the last five years that law enforcement has realized that what happens on the inside can affect what happens on the outside and vice versa."

Of the two kinds of gangs, prison gangs and street gangs, the prison gangs are better organized, according to gang investigators. They developed within the prison system in California, Texas and Illinois in the 1940s and are low-key, discreet—even stealthy. They monitor members and dictate how they behave and treat each other. A serious violation means death, say investigators.

The street gangs are more flagrant. "Their members are going into the prisons and realizing that one of the reasons they are in prison is that they kept such a high profile" making it easier for the police to catch them, says Buentello. "So, they are coming out more sophisticated and more dangerous because they aren't as easily detected. They also network and keep track of who is out and so forth."

According to gang investigators and prisoners, the prison gangs were formed for protection against predatory inmates, but racketeering, black markets and racism became factors.

Godwin says Texas should never have outlawed smoking in the prisons, adding cigarettes as trade-goods contraband to the prohibited list. "If you go back to the Civil War era, to Andersonville prison," Godwin says of the prisoner-of-war facility for Union soldiers, "you will see that the first thing that developed was a gang because someone had to control the contraband—that is power. I'm convinced that if you put three people on an island somewhere, two would clique up and become predatory against the other at some point."

But protection remains an important factor. When a new inmate enters the prison system he is challenged to a fight, according to a Texas state-pen prisoner. The outcome determines who can fight, who will be extorted for protection money and who will become a servant to other prisoners. Those who can't join a gang or afford to spend $5 a week in commissary items for protection are destined to be servants. Godwin explains: "The environment is set up so that when you put that many people with antisocial behavior and criminal history together, someone is going to be the predator and someone the prey, and that is reality."

The Texas inmate describes a system in which gangs often recruit like fraternities, targeting short-term inmates because they can help the gang—pay them back, so to speak—when they leave prison for the free world. Most of the groups thrive on lifelong membership, according to the Florida DC, with "blood in, blood out" oaths extending leadership and membership beyond the prison into the lucrative drug trade, extortion and pressure rackets.

Prison gangs operating in Texas and Florida include Neta, the Texas Syndicate, the Aztecs, the Mexican Mafia, the New Black Panthers, the Black Guerrilla Family, Mandingo Warriors, Aryan Brotherhood, La Nuestra Familia, the Aryan Circle and the White Knights. Some of these gangs have alliances, and some are mortal enemies. Many on this list originated in California over the decades, some of them (such as the Texas Syndicate) to protect members from the other gangs. In addition, street gangs such as the Crips and Bloods and traditional racial-hate groups such as the Ku Klux Klan also operate in the prisons.

The Reaction from Law Enforcement Officials

What prisoners may not realize is that because the gangs are monitored by prison authorities the law-enforcement community is becoming very sophisticated about the gangs. "Sixty percent of what we learn about what is going on in the city streets of Florida" is garnered in prison and not from observing the streets, says Godwin.

Prison officials say they concentrate on inmate behavior to identify gang members. They do not single out gang leaders to strike any deals because acknowledging the gang as anything other than a "security-threat group" gives them too much credibility. This has been a particular problem in Puerto Rico with the native and political Neta gang.

Recognizing groups during the 1970s, in a system in which prisoners have the right to vote, has led to a tendency among politicians to award clemency to some inmates.

Officials in Texas have reacted most stringently to gang members. They isolate and place them in lockdown status to discourage membership. Buentello says this approach has produced a dramatic decrease in violence. In 1984, 53 inmates were killed due to gang violence. After the new policy was implemented in 1985, homicides dropped to five and then continued to decline.

Godwin says Florida uses a closed-management system that only locks up prisoners for 23 hours, with further enforcement based on inmate behavior.

"The reality is they are going to be able to get away with doing things when we have only a handful of prison staff," Godwin cautions, adding that the system needs to increase the professionalism of the staff with pay raises and training. Many employees are recruited out of the same neighborhoods as the prisoners, he explains.

Linda Washburn of the Massachusetts Department of Corrections, a much smaller system than Texas or Florida, says her state handles prisoner gangs just like Florida. According to her, size doesn't matter when it comes to prison-gang problems because no one is immune to it. "This issue crosses so many lines in society and in the prisons that it requires us in law enforcement and criminal justice to unite and confront the issue together . . . as a team with one voice."

It isn't about bad guys killing bad guys. It's about drug dealers and racketeers profiting off the system. And Godwin warns that the direct effect on American neighborhoods is realized when the 16-year-old sent up for 25 years gets paroled and moves in next door.

NONTRADITIONAL GANGS

Steven L. Sachs

Counselor and judicial officer Steven L. Sachs has worked extensively with gang members and other delinquent youths since beginning his career at a juvenile detention center in 1978. He has served as a juvenile probation officer, juvenile detentions counselor, home detention officer, and bond supervision officer in Lake County, Illinois. In the following excerpt from his book *Street Gang Awareness: A Resource Guide for Parents and Professionals*, Sachs provides an overview of gangs that vary from the traditional structure, membership, or purpose of most gangs. In particular, he outlines the origins and traits of skinhead gangs and tagger gangs.

Skinhead gangs got their foothold in America during the mid-1980s, but their history can be traced back to England in the 1960s. In many small towns in Great Britain at that time, high unemployment along with a growing influx of immigrants from developing countries caused youths to become fearful. They feared they were being edged out of the job market, and saw the immigrants as a threat to the white working class. This fear grew into the intense hatred and extreme nationalism that pervade Skinhead gangs today. The hatred of the new immigrants spilled over to include Jews and other minorities as well.

The Skinheads' manner and style of dress was formulated at that time to reflect their working-class roots. The term "skinhead" refers to the practice of gang members shaving their heads, which they did to avoid having their hair pulled during physical confrontations with police or pedestrians.

The music of the sixties also played a part in the growth and identification of the skinhead movement. Skinhead music—yes, there are specific music groups just for Skinheads—gradually became known as "Oi" [pronounced like the "oi" in "oil" and meaning "us versus them"]. Skinheads use this word in Europe and the United States as a universal greeting to one another.

Today's Skinheads come from all income levels; they may be male or female. They frequently have academic problems, use excessive amounts of drugs or alcohol, and many are victims of physical or sexual abuse. Skinheads hate all types of authority. They tend to be "loners," often feeling alienated from family, society, and the government. Alienated individuals are at a greater risk of being recruited into the Skinhead movement, because they hope to gain superiority and power through intimidation.

Over the last two decades, the American Skinhead movement has established ties with more traditional white supremacy groups, such as the Ku Klux Klan and the Aryan Nation. Along with these alliances comes a more extreme ideology, as well as a more intense hatred and prejudice toward minorities, gays, and Jews.

Skinhead Subdivisions

The Skinheads themselves are splintered into two different factions; the Racists and the Antiracists. Racists, the most narrowly-focused individuals, are made up of three different subgroups: White Power, White Pride, and White Supremacy. The White Supremacy gang, over the years, has been given the names Boot Boys, Hammerskins, Nazi Skins, LADS (L.A. Death Squad), The Northern Hammer Skins, the WAY, the ORDER, and Hitler Youth. The difference between the three subgroups lies in the intensity and commitment each displays. They are the hard-core members. Their philosophy states that all people of color are inferior, and that race mixing and homosexuality are abominations to God and country and should be stopped by any means necessary. They also believe that Jews control all financial institutions, media, and governments worldwide.

While African American, Hispanic, and Southeast Asian gangs are motivated by money, the goal of Racist Skinheads is to spread hate. They do this through public demonstrations, literature, and graffiti. Racists view themselves as the white working class and claim that it was their white fathers and forefathers who built this nation. The achievements and contributions of other groups are considered insignificant and often looked upon with disdain.

As Racist Skinheads started to emerge in this country, the second, smaller group of Skinheads, the Antiracist Skinheads, began to evolve. Antiracists have a multiracial membership, but adhere to the same style of dress, haircut, and preference in music as the Racists. The Antiracist view, however, is that everyone is equal and should not be discriminated against because of skin color, religion, or heritage. This difference has resulted in many bloody brawls between the Antiracists and Racists. Antiracist gangs have a variety of names, each promoting the idea of racial harmony: Mud Skins, Two-Tone Skins, and Racial Unity Skinheads. The most widely known Antiracist gang is Skinheads Against Racial Prejudice, or SHARP. In the eighties, SHARP had a reputation of being more prone to violence than other gangs, and many Antiracist Skinheads disassociated themselves from the group.

Tagger Gangs

Tagger gangs, sometimes called crews, cliques, or posses, have been around for a number of years. Taggers are graffiti artists; the city is their canvas. Tagger gangs are generally made up of teens who use spray paint, felt pens, and paint brushes. Their artwork—which police and city officials call vandalism—can be found on buildings and city walls, in subways and parking garages, on water towers, on train station platforms, and on the sides of trains. Trains are especially prized by Taggers; their artwork rolls out from the train station early in the morning to thousands of ready-made art patrons (daily commuters). Railroad personnel scramble to keep up with Taggers, covering the artwork with heavy solvents.

Taggers will spend days putting their ideas down on paper, making rough sketches and assigning colors to patterns. Then, under the cover of night, Taggers will spend eight to ten hours painting the side of a train. Their artwork can be intricate, colorful, and complex. Their names will usually accompany the graffiti. All that work for a week's worth of glory, at most.

While traditional gangs are often amazed by Taggers' artwork, there are times when conflicts arise. Because Taggers create their artwork wherever they feel like it, turf boundaries are sometimes violated. Traditional gangs have been known to retaliate against Tagger gangs, which has led some Taggers to join other traditional gangs for protection. There are also incidents where one Tagger gang has intentionally painted over another's artwork, leading to violence as Tagger gangs attempt to claim territory. Some Taggers now carry weapons to their painting sites.

Taggers are proud of their artwork. They take photographs of their graffiti, knowing that their work will be short-lived. Taggers often place these photographs in an album, much the same way a new mother puts photos of her newborn child in a family scrapbook. They keep these graffiti "portfolios" as trophies to show to other Taggers. Some years back, there was a television movie about a graffiti Tagger. Despite the usual plot relating violent confrontations and a breakdown of family dynamics, this story had an unusual ending. A caring social worker, seeing the potential in this misguided Tagger, had him show his photo album to a corporate executive, who hired the young teenager as a beginning graphic artist.

A reality check, if you please. Taggers, for the most part write their graffiti for the sheer excitement of it, and for their own gratification. As a bridge to future employment? I don't think so. Graffiti costs American taxpayers untold millions of dollars each year, and most businesses are unforgiving of such vandalism.

PROFILE OF A SUBURBAN GANGSTER

Dan Korem

> Although the ranks of traditional gangs have been filled largely
> with minority youths from urban ghetto areas, in recent years
> gang activity has begun to spread to the suburbs. Alienated
> white teenagers—often from broken homes—are attracted to
> gangs as a way of finding status, identity, and acceptance. In the
> following selection from his book *Suburban Gangs—The Affluent
> Rebels*, investigative journalist and author Dan Korem presents
> the experiences of one such suburban gangster, Andy Joseph
> Kriz of Minnesota. As Korem explains, Kriz originally joined a
> traditional inner-city gang, but he soon formed his own multi-
> racial gang, headquartered in his suburban neighborhood.

The kid could have been anybody, but not long ago he felt like
nobody—an outsider. He sounded like a lot of kids growing up in
America's heartland. Where he lived was not quite Norman Rockwell's
idealized, American town, but it certainly wasn't the urban, nightmar-
ish underbelly often flashed across America's television screens during
evening news broadcasts. But if you listened closely, you heard a dead
edge to his voice: *"In my home I was a nobody. I hated it. When I was
young, I was fat until the seventh grade, and kids bothered me because of
my attention deficit disorder. I got in all kinds of fights with kids who were
making fun of me."*

Gang Violence Hits the Heartland

Residents of Minneapolis-St. Paul, the Twin Cities, use words like
"nice" and "clean" when they affectionately refer to their city. Yet in
this benign, seemingly innocent place, the nobody's path crossed the
path of a nice, law-abiding, law-enforcing man. Jerry Haaf was a nice
guy, who worked the streets. People didn't think that gangs would
invade a smaller, more isolated metropolitan area like theirs. Big cities
like Chicago, Dallas, Los Angeles, New York City, and Miami—yes!
Minneapolis-St. Paul? No. Inner-city gang violence was commonplace
in *other* places, but not in the Twin Cities, home of the 1991 World
Series champs.

On September 24, 1992, Officer Haaf met a nobody hell-bent on becoming a somebody—or at least he met the nobody's bullets. He was gunned down—shot in the back—while in a pizza shop in a run-down section of south Minneapolis.

The same night, another nobody was arrested. Andy Joseph Kriz, formerly of New Brighton, a suburb filled with $100,000–$250,000 homes, was taken into custody. As far as the police were concerned, he was somebody—somebody dangerous. He was the leader of the DFL (Down For Life) gang. He was ostensibly arrested for an unrelated shooting of several members of the Latin King gang in north Min-neapolis. These shootings awakened people. They started talking about gangs, even in the suburbs.

Andy Kriz's parents divorced when he was young. Both remarried, but Andy never got along with his step-father; and he never saw his real father on a regular basis until he was eighteen—the same year he started serving time at St. Cloud Penitentiary, a massive one-hundred-year-old granite prison. Inmates called it the Greystone College—Gladiator School . . . a place you have to prove yourself.

Andy: *"Gangs were something I could relate to for once. When I was liv-ing in New Brighton, all these other kids had two parents . . . they cared what happened and could buy their kids stuff. I couldn't relate to any of them. I wanted power over the pain inside of me."*

In 1986, when twelve years old, he was with his father for the first time since he was three. The same year Andy started hanging out with the G.D.—Gangster Disciples, which were under the umbrella of the Folks nation of gangs—he would visit his father in a deteriorating neighborhood in north Minneapolis. He was also fascinated by the Vice Lords, the same gang that later shot and killed Officer Haaf.

Andy: *"I was fascinated how nobody bothered them. They stuck together like a group [unlike his parents]. They were like a family. But that's only a part of it. They had money. But it's an excuse. Your excuse is that you are hungry. But your greed grows, because greed always grows.*

"Gangs are so pretty at first, so shiny. But it just turns into hell. I remem-ber how much fun I used to have gang-banging. You didn't live by any rules, whatsoever . . . but then it got bad. It wasn't fun anymore."

Andy was put in rehab for drug use when he was fourteen. The fol-lowing year he joined the Gangster Disciples. *"The initiation lasted six minutes. Six guys beat you and you couldn't fall or say anything."*

Forming His Own Gang

Dealing drugs, breaking in and stealing from New Brighton homes, and ripping off were a part of the routine. By the time he was seven-teen, Andy left the Disciples and formed his own gang, Down For Life—DFL. He recruited three youths he met in drug rehab and one from the neighborhood where his father lived. It was a racially mixed gang—white, Hispanic, and a Native American Indian. Each came from broken homes where the mother headed the household.

Andy: *"Our sign was a four-pointed crown. Each point stood for pride, power, protection, and partnership. Joining our gang was a lifetime commitment."*

By the summer of 1991, over twenty-five youths had been recruited. Andy could buy anything he wanted, eat out at restaurants, and regularly carried at least $500 in his pocket. Then the Latin Kings tried to invade his New Brighton turf. He moved again from New Brighton to the north end of Minneapolis, but DLF's turf was still New Brighton.

"I was walking up Tenth Avenue to Broadway going to Burger King. I had been drinking. A car stopped and four Latin Kings jumped out. We fought and they stabbed me in my arm, chest, and the back of my head. It took me a couple of months to figure out that the house was at 18th and Taylor. So we drove by the house once and the second time we circled by, they all came out on the street. That's when I started shooting."

Andy pumped three rounds into the crowd from his 12-gauge shotgun. Three people received only minor wounds, but a fourth Latin King was sprayed in the face and chest. He later recovered.

"We then took off, rented the movie Lawnmower Man *and watched it at the apartment of one of our girlfriends."*

Facing the Consequences

A short while later, the Minneapolis PD descended on the apartment, arresting everyone. Andy denied the shooting, but was convicted of the shooting and robbery. He was sentenced to six years.

Lt. Bob Jacobson, one of the officers who worked Andy's case and a youth gang specialist, said, "Andy's really a good kid. I think he's got better than a 50/50 chance of making it when he gets out." He based his assessment on talks he had had with Andy since the time he was fifteen.

He observed that virtually every youth involved in gang activity came from a broken home. When asked what he thought would be the most effective deterrent to gang activity, he said: *"Stabilizing the home. If that doesn't work, go to prison. It's about the only thing that will scare them."*

Andy agreed. He said,

"Nothing would have worked for me to stop. There's nothing you could really do. I have a sister, right now, who joined the Latin Kings. I've tried talking her out it. But she's just like I was." Since he started serving his sentence in January of 1992, he has burned the bridges with his gang, earned his GED, and is now on the honor unit. Special privileges include: being out of his cell twelve hours a day, better food, and a separate store and weight room. He adds,

"I'd rather be the geekiest person on the streets than the coolest sucker in prison. You can stay out of trouble when you don't feel you have to get respect—being a man shooting someone. My emotional mentality is only now just starting to grow because of what I did."

CHAPTER 3

LIFE IN A GANG

THE FUNCTIONS OF GANG VIOLENCE

Alan McEvoy, Edsel Erickson, and Norman Randolph

In the following excerpt from their book Youth Gangs: Guidelines for Educators and Community Youth Leaders, *Alan McEvoy, Edsel Erickson, and Norman Randolph explore the myriad functions of gang violence. According to the authors, violence is an integral part of many ritualistic elements—such as the initiation of new recruits—that are used to strengthen the bonds between gang members. McEvoy is a professor of sociology at Wittenberg University in Springfield, Ohio. Erickson is the executive director of the Safe Schools Coalition, which works to reduce violence and promote health and safety in schools. The assistant superintendent of the West Mifflin Area School District in Pennsylvania, Randolph has developed several intervention programs for gang members.*

The late model van with tinted windows posed no obvious threat as it cruised the streets adjacent to campus. It was nearly three in the morning on a weekend; there would be late parties and drunken students walking home. There, on a poorly lit side street, were two male college students. No one else was in sight. As the van approached and slowed, the students seemed oblivious to the impending danger. No doubt both had consumed too much alcohol. Perfect.

Without warning, the driver of the van hit the breaks and cut the lights. Out jumped six young men—members of the local affiliate of the Vice Lords—and surrounded the two students. Each gang member was armed. The four older members formed an outside ring. The two new recruits, who were being initiated into the gang, confronted the students. One of the new recruits held a knife, the other a pistol. Both were apprehensive about fulfilling their required task.

The older gang members said nothing. They had instructed the young recruits to show their stuff without help. In a nervous voice, one of the young recruits demanded the students' wallets. The surprised and frightened victims acquiesced without saying a word. Then the young gangsters demanded that the students take off their shoes. It was freezing and wet. One student instantly began to comply but the other student paused and offered mild verbal resistance. He said, "C'mon, man, it's cold . . . give me a break."

As if that was the needed cue, the young man with the knife cursed, then slashed the student in the arm. Blood gushed as he cried in pain and toppled to the ground. Hovering over the injured student with knife in hand, the young gangster said, "Mother f - - - er, you lose your thumb if you talk like that again." The bleeding student began to cry.

The other student also fell to the ground and said, " Please, please, don't hurt us." He was told to "shut the f - - - up." But both students did what most would do—they continued to ask for mercy. Angered, the two young gang members began to kick them in the ribs, the genitals, and finally in the face. Although nearly senseless with pain and fear, one student managed to say, "Oh God, please don't do this anymore." Then the young man with the pistol screamed, "I said shut the f - - - up," as he shot twice.

The first bullet grazed one student along the side of his face, severing a portion of his ear—a near miss that could have killed him. The other student was shot in the knee; he was lucky to escape death, but unlucky in that he would be permanently handicapped. As a finale to the event, both of the injured, bleeding students were kicked several more times by the new recruits. Then all six gang members jumped into the van and sped off. The victims would remain bleeding for another 10 minutes before help arrived.

As the van slowed and blended with traffic, no one said anything for several minutes. Finally, the driver of the van—a senior gang member—said, "Let's see the wallets." The combined cash total was $27; the driver pocketed the money. When the gang members returned to their home turf, approximately a dozen of their peers awaited them. The driver of the van scanned the group, smiled, and said, "They did good." With that accomplished, the new recruits awaited their final rite of passage into the gang—being beaten by those who would then embrace them as full members—if they survived.

Seeking the Reasons Behind the Insanity

In considering this cruel scenario, one is left to ponder basic questions: How could these young people be so heartless and cruel? How could two young teenagers, who presumably would not have considered committing such brutality a few years earlier, transform so quickly into vicious, cold-blooded thugs?

The motives behind the brutal battery of the two college students seem senseless—at least from a perspective that respects human life. To be disdainful of such violence, however, does not mean there are no reasons behind this brutality.

In a sense, gang violence is a communal event—rather like a ritual— linking members together in a common bond. They use violence to initiate new members into the gang. They share together the danger and the excitement of violence directed toward outsiders, they provide cover for one another, and they share events in stories that are passed on in an oral tradition. These are the ritual-like elements that help to create deep bonds of loyalty. By engaging in violence in the company of one another the gang causes its members to feel that their violence is normal, creating a subcultural dynamic that takes on a momentum of its own. The gang culture, with all its traditions and rituals, constitutes a whole which is greater than the sum of its constituent individual participants.

Thus, it is the power of the gang to motivate, direct, and positively sanction violence by its members that must be an object of our understanding. . . .

The reasons behind the violence of gangs are many—some obvious, others more subtle and latent. Particularly in low income areas, brutality is used most obviously in youth gangs to:

- defend or expand the gang's turf,
- recruit or "jump in" new members,
- keep members from leaving,
- exclude or "jump out" undesirable members,
- exercise revenge or seek redress for perceived wrongs to the gang,
- enhance perceptions of the gang's power and invincibility,
- gain respect or dominance over others,
- enforce rules, and
- serve as a counterpoint or check on what some might call moral restraints or a moral conscience.

Regarding this last point, in the gang culture moral restraints on violent impulses are seen as dysfunctional. If the gang demands that a member engage in swift and certain violence, it would simply be too risky to have the person pause and engage in moral equivocation about the appropriateness of the violence. The more one responds to the peer pressure to be violent, the less one feels moral restraint, and the more one develops a kind of "psychic numbing" regarding acts of brutality. That is why, over time, even extreme acts of brutality, such as murder, can occur with the perpetrators not only failing to show remorse, but to the contrary, exhibiting pride in their violent actions.

Bonding and Violence

Not as obvious, gang violence and its consequence—the constant threat of violence—have other important unstated functions, including strengthening gang members' attachments to one another (i.e., bonding). In turn, this bonding provides a basis for further violence, and the cycle of violence continues.

Violence does many things to a gang as a group entity, not the least is its tendency to bring the members together. Sharing the anticipation, danger, harm, and excitement of a gang's exercise of brutality against outsiders creates feelings of common identity and shared purpose, as was illustrated in the attack on college students by adolescents being initiated into a gang. The recruits who actually conducted the violence, the leaders who ordered and observed the violence, and those who were later told that the recruits "did good," were all sharing in the violence—they all felt somewhat united as a result of the violent actions of just two recruits.

It was not, however, the viciousness of the attack or the amount of time the recruits took to savage the college students that was most relevant for affecting feelings of togetherness. In fact, as a bonding agent, the occasional occurrence of violence can go a long way as episodes of fear and rage are relived, exaggerated, and contemplated. This is clear from the small amount of time spent on violence by even the most violent gangs. Violent acts are relatively limited as compared to the time gang members spend contemplating violence or the threat of violence. In research reported by the Bureau of Justice Assistance only 10 percent or less of the memberships of gangs are composed of hard-core, violent members.

Furthermore, research by the Bureau of Justice Assistance supports the view that "most gang members are, with the exception of members of wilding gangs, only peripherally involved in violence; and most importantly only a small percentage of gang members account for most of the harm done by their gangs." Yet there is a considerable impact on bonding among all gang members from even the rarest amount of gang-generated violence.

Forging a Common Identity

The bonding effect on gang members when gang violence occurs is similar to that occurring in large communities and nations. Members of the military, for instance, who experience combat tend to develop feelings of common identity; as do many civilians who identify with the military. The violent battles of the Civil War, which lasted only hours, are reenacted over and over again, year after year, reinforcing a Confederate or Union identity. Clearly, occasional acts of group violence define group boundaries, create or reinforce group identities, and bind members together in a common cause. Yet it is the shared vicarious reconstruction or anticipation of violence that is so much more relevant to bonding than is violence per se. In a sense, the violence serves a symbolic purpose: it represents group solidarity and group identity.

The relevance of the vicarious experience of violence can be observed in many other common situations. When people visit the Holocaust Museum in Washington, D.C., they are mortified when they see pictures of what was done to people in the German concentration camps of World War II. With most visitors of both Jewish and Gentile persuasion there tends to occur a shared experience of compassion. The compassion is for victims of human brutality more than a half-century ago. These experiences of compassion are part of the glue of bonding—a glue that attaches victims to victims, nonvictims to victims, and nonvictims to one another.

It is immaterial whether individuals are really or vicariously the perpetrators or victims of violence as far as bonding taking place. Entire religious and cultural communities have been strengthened in part by shared feelings of others being victimized or being persecuted.

This is analogous to military personnel who bond together when faced with adversity and external threat, or police officers who work together through a riot. The ethic is clear: the more you have enemies, the more you have to trust and rely upon your fellow gang members for protection, and the more you have to use violent means to assure safety.

When this principle is applied to gangs we understand why—when the police, school authorities, alien gangs, or others harass or attack a gang—they strengthen the bond the gang members have for each other. Gang members then feel that they are being victimized. The harassment thereby causes more problems for authorities as they attempt to suppress gang violence or other crimes. The gang becomes more united and resistant to pressures of change. Furthermore, harassment of a gang may cause it to grow in size and gain some respectability within the larger culture—which causes additional problems for society. . . .

Cultural Values

There are, of course, both psychological and social forces behind any act of gang-initiated violence. Of the social norms operating within many groups—and particularly in gangs—is a force created by the juxtaposition of four highly touted cultural values that support the use of violence to solve problems. These are the cultural values of courage, heroism, machismo, and physical prowess. Gang members give great importance to being viewed by their peers as courageous, willing to be heroes if need be, being "properly" masculine (and we might add that even female gangs are adopting certain traits that traditionally have been considered masculine), and being strong and not a "wimp." Maintaining some semblance of social order is another cultural value that most gang members hold, but like the other values they tend not to know how to achieve order except through the use of violence.

It may seem strange to view gang members as heroic or courageous, but from their perspective the phenomenon is the same as individuals earning combat awards from their nation for their courageousness under fire. An enemy soldier who loses his life in defense of his country is seldom seen as being courageous or a hero; except, that is, by that soldier's nation—the enemy. This is the case with society viewing gang members who risk their lives for their gangs, and vice versa gang members viewing the police who risk their lives in defense of societal values.

Just as in the military, gang violence is planned, anticipated, experienced, and relived, and the concepts of courage and heroism shape discussion. The virtues of courage and heroism are used in justifying violence for defensive or expansion purposes, or for any one of the long list of reasons given above. For a gang member to defy family, friends, authorities, and other gangs in order to serve his or her gang is to sacrifice certain respect from others and to even be punished or killed, but to gain the respect of the gang. Giving up something to be a gang member is looked upon as courageous. The more the risk of being personally harmed in the service of the gang, the more that courage is attributed by the other gang members. And those who are hurt or exhibit extraordinary risk of being hurt are seen as heroes; i.e., they exhibit courage far beyond the usual expected service to the gang.

Thus, society has another problem in dealing with gangs that is not easily solved. Gang members highly prize identities connected to being courageous; yet for them, courage and heroism often can only be achieved through the occasional exhibition of illegal violence. That is one reason why violence plays such a major role in the gang culture.

The Function of Machismo

There are other group values and norms that are related to gang-initiated violence, particularly by male gangs. One is a variation of machismo—a value favoring the dominance of males over females, and that females are rightly subject to male exploitation and reprimand without any need for compassion. In such group circumstances the exhibition of violence against females is not disdained and is even seen as demonstrating manliness. When such norms exist in a gang, gang rape and other brutishness toward females can easily occur.

There is a related macho value that emphasizes the primacy of "manly strength" over being a "wimp." When this value is exercised, bullying behavior and beating up on weaker individuals—both males and females—is endorsed. Unfortunately, this can even become a sport, particularly of "wilding" gangs.

While not all male gangs are characterized by norms justifying the use of physical violence against women and "wimpy" males, nearly all male gangs have machismo as a core norm; that is, the dominance of males over females and the importance of manly strength—a cultural trait in varying degrees throughout much of the world. However, when coupled with certain other norms of gang cultures, machismo can spark the worst forms of sexual violence.

Even gangs opposed as a group to the battering and rape of women may tolerate gang members who are violent toward women and others outside of their roles as gang members; that is, if there are no costs to the gang as a group. Gangs often view such violence as a personal matter and not a gang activity. In other words, gangs that do not endorse violence against women do not always impede such violence by their members when it is done apart from gang activity.

Some gangs, particularly when they reach the entrepreneurial stage, set clear limits on when, how, and where its members may or must be violent. This is one reason that unprovoked violence by gang members often lessens when gangs become more highly organized and engaged in illicit businesses—random and personal violence is simply bad for business. For these gangs, violence is to be used sparingly and judiciously for salient rational gang and leadership purposes. In such gangs, violence is mostly used for control by punishing members and external targets who get out of line. The more successful gangs know that the threat of violence is far more effective in controlling others than violence per se.

For the individual gang member the cultural norm of being in control in a setting characterized by threat and danger poses two special problems. First, each member must consider violence as a means of achieving or maintaining status in his or her gang. Second, each member is likely to see violence as the only way of avoiding or reducing embarrassment, harm, threat, or loss of control over self; i.e., of avoiding the consequences of being viewed as a "wimp."

Violence for Leadership or Prestige

There are three main ways of achieving authority or prestige in a gang. One is through wit and cleverness that produces benefits for the gang. Another is through sponsorship by gang leaders. Some gangs use the term "blessed" to reflect this sponsorship. And one is through the demonstration of the power to inflict harm on others for any insult or any resistance to one's demands. The Bureau of Justice Assistance reports that only about 10 percent of most street gangs are made up of hard-core leaders. It is the leaders who tend to be the most violent members in each gang; they aggressively threaten others and in so doing maintain their leadership roles.

Added to the willingness of leaders to personally act violently is the ability to cause other gang members to be violent as instructed. Gang leaders often cause rank-and-file gang members or recruits, who would otherwise not be so inclined, to engage in particularly violent actions. And those who would be so inclined are limited and directed in their violence. In fact, it is through ordering others to carry out violent actions that leaders gain maximum power. From highly organized crime families to local street gangs, the top leaders tend to have a history where they once exercised considerable violence themselves, but now primarily direct others' violence.

Whether acting violently or directing others to be violent, gang leadership requires an occasional demonstration of violence. This is because the threat of violence is at the heart of gang leadership. For the leadership in some gangs, violence may take the form of personally killing or ordering the execution of a gang member who has violated a gang norm, killing an outsider, or a ritualistic drive-by shooting. At a less violent level, physical abuse may be administered. Two gangs in Chicago illustrate such differences in the use of violence. In one, for example, if a member disputes the leadership's request, an order to be executed is almost automatic. In this gang, if two rank-and-file gang members have a serious dispute with one another and do not resolve it themselves, the leaders are likely to order the execution of one of the disputants. In another gang, executions are rarely ordered to settle conflicts among its members. Rather, after a hearing, one or several disputants may be subjected to extremely intense beatings. In both of these Chicago gangs, nonetheless, violence and the threat of violence are the keys to the gang leaders' control.

Because of the violence required of gang leadership, for the rank and file there are few ways of displacing leadership except through extreme violence. Rarely does merely threatening a leader cause him or her to give up authority. While sometimes a subordinate gang member may report a leader to law enforcement for some crime as a way of getting rid of a leader, this method seldom achieves status in a gang. Such action will seldom receive the endorsement of the gang members—for a "snitch" can never be trusted. On the other hand, violence is an accepted form for anyone to use to achieve power, while squealing is one of the worst sins of the gang culture. The ability and willingness to exercise violence, therefore, is sort of the "coin of the realm" as far as gaining or maintaining gang leadership.

To be violent, however, carries with it many risks—even to the leadership. Victims may wait for the time to get even. Revenge is a strong and lasting motive in the gang culture. Thus, for a gang leader to insult or attack someone who has the ability to respond with an even greater imposition of harm would be to reduce one's status and power—a foolish act even in a gang. There is the inclination among gang leaders and would-be leaders to seek out those who are perceived to be weak or unwilling to strike back. They need to demonstrate courage and violence on those who are vulnerable. Of course, the norms of the gang culture, as in most other groups and nations, support the view that it is only advisable to attack others under conditions of minimal danger to self. Thus, guns displace fists and chains as weapons of choice in many gangs. The idea is pick on someone who does not have the firepower or the willingness to strike back.

Using Violence to Reduce Threat

Obviously the norm of using violence against those who are weaker has a reciprocal impact on potential victims. As reported by the Justice Department, there has been a large increase in the number of guns in the hands of nongang members in gang areas. In fact, there are more guns owned by nongang youth than there are among gang members. These nongang members claim they need guns for purposes of defense, often against gangs. However, they create major problems for themselves and authorities. Further, these potential victims carrying guns are, in turn, a threat to the gangs and cause the gangs to arm themselves even more. As a result many communities have an "arms race."

For the individual rank-and-file gang member, the importance of violence for survival also shapes reactions. The logic here is simple. In the street-gang culture, the world is a hostile place. The gang member, as well as the nongang member, is often vulnerable to attack from any quarter, at almost any time, with little warning or provocation. In such a climate there is always someone willing to take advantage of someone who is weak. As such, a type of cost-benefit analysis of responding to any insult or threat operates. Failure to let aggressors know that retaliation will occur if insulted or assaulted may be viewed as more costly and dangerous than the actual risk of striking back. To fail to retaliate is to have others see oneself as weak and thus invite continual victimization.

According to this gang-culture norm, gang members run a special risk of disrespect and victimization by their leadership and peers if they fail to violently respond to the slightest insult or threat from anyone other than their leadership—and even here, submission to victimization invites further victimization. As perceived in the gang culture, confronting violence with violence has two benefits: it gains respect and it reduces the risk of further victimization in the long run.

GANGS IN CYBERSPACE

Karen Kaplan

Gangs have traditionally battled over the territorial boundaries that separate one neighborhood from another. With the rise of the Internet, however, gangs are also starting to claim turf in cyberspace, as journalist Karen Kaplan describes in the following selection. Many gangs have begun to create their own websites, according to the author, and these sites are often characterized by the same territorial warfare that occurs in real life, with rival gang members trying to hack into the sites to deface them with graffiti. Law enforcement officials also view these websites with concern, worrying that gangsters will use them to sell illegal drugs online. However, she points out, some sites reveal a softer side of gang life by including thoughtful poetry and tributes to deceased friends. Kaplan is a staff writer for the *Los Angeles Times*.

Anthony, a brawny Sacramento teenager who hangs with the Nortenos street gang, was casually surfing the Web one day and was stunned when he stumbled on a smattering of home pages posted by members of the Sureno gang, the Nortenos' sworn and sometimes bloody rival.

It became a matter of pride for Anthony, an 18-year-old high school graduate, to learn enough about building a Web site to represent his gang online.

"NORTENOS!" blares his SacTown Gangstas Web site, decorated with pictures of a modified United Farm Workers logo, a gleaming red Impala, an automatic pistol, two pit bull terriers and a cheery Web button inviting visitors to "e-mail me."

"I'm doing it for all the Nortenos that are uneducated on the computer," said Anthony, who declined to give his last name because he fears reprisals from police. "They live through me."

Gangs Invade the Internet

Real-world street gang turf wars have spread to cyberspace. The result has been a host of unexpected consequences for law enforcement, gang members and even corporate advertisers, who have found themselves unwitting sponsors.

Excerpted from "Gangs Finding New Turf," by Karen Kaplan, *Los Angeles Times*, May 31, 2001. Copyright © 2001 by *Los Angeles Times*. Reprinted with permission.

"There are literally thousands of gang-related Web sites," said Chuck Zeglin, a Los Angeles police detective who monitors online gang activity. "I've been dealing with gangs for 17 years, and two years ago we never would have expected any type of gang member to be sophisticated enough to get on the Internet."

"Yeah, gangbangers *do* know how to use a computer," replied Mr. Bandit, an 18-year-old Web master from the Mid City Stoners 13 gang in Los Angeles who declined to give his real name. "Gangbangers do got talents."

The emergence of gang sites is largely a phenomenon of the last year, driven by plummeting computer prices, easy Internet access and the proliferation of companies offering free space on the Web.

Internet search engines indicate there are thousands of gang-themed Web sites, although experts say a significant portion of them are run by basically strait-laced kids who simply think the gang lifestyle is cool. Dozens of the most appealing Web addresses—including *http://www.bloods.com, http://www.crips.com,* and *http://www.latinkings.com* —belong to a self-described "former slum lord" in the Missouri Ozarks who is crusading to steer at-risk youths away from gang life.

The gang sites are part high school yearbook, part church eulogy for departed friends and part art gallery of airbrushed cars, naked women and various semiautomatic weapons. Images of sign-flashing gang members and prized weapons collections adorn the sites like the snapshots of needlepoint patterns and family pets on other Web sites.

Claiming Online Turf

Although there are no street corners or neighborhoods to fight over, the virtual turf of the online world has become just as precious as any real-world block for young gang members who have grown up with the Internet.

The gangs have transformed their tiny corners of the Internet into a kind of infinite electronic swath of freeway overpasses and railroad trestles waiting to be marked by the techno version of spray-painted gang tags.

"We're taking over your [neighborhoods] and you can't do [anything] about it," reads a message posted by a Sureno on the Land of the Nortenos site. "What's up with those fools thinking they're hard with those cap guns, what are we supposed to be, scared?"

The Nortenos fired back with a torrent of expletives. "The big NORTE will always put it down on you punk RATS. You can't fade OR EVEN HANG WITH THE PURO NORTH SIDE MAFIA!"

On rare occasions, gang members escalate the conflict by hacking into each other's sites. One of the victims was a Surena with the moniker "Mz. Smiley."

"Well due to some haters who . . . hacked into mah page and well my site is gonna be down," is all her site says now.

But in a realm where no real blood has ever been spilled, the gang sites also show a different side of street life often obscured in the harsh bluster of crime reports and gangsta rap. Here, young artists recount the pain of first love. They sing the praises of ancient Chevrolets and pit bulls amid pages adorned with kewpie-like couples exchanging flowers.

On Anthony's site, one poet wrote:

No one could ever hurt me quite as much as you,
When I said I loved, every word I spoke was true.
Now I'm feeling brokedown, cold and alone . . . not
Knowing what to do, left only with memories.

"A lot of people, they think that gang members are bad, but not all of them are," said Edwin, a Sureno with a Web site named Puro Brown Pride, which has links to dozens of drawings reflecting both the "madness and the sadness" of gang life.

In many ways, the gang sites are a sign of the crumbling digital divide. Already, more than 50% of American homes have computers. For the young, access is even easier, given the number of computers in schools, libraries and workplaces. The Internet has become as natural a part of life for young gang members as television, cars and beepers were to an earlier generation.

So far, most of the gangs' online activity is perfectly legal. It isn't against the law to belong to a gang, nor is it illegal to discuss one's gang affiliations on the Net.

But the quick spread of gang sites has put law enforcement on alert. The Drug Enforcement Administration is putting together a unit focused on online gang activity.

"They're just testing the waters now, but it's inevitable" that gangs will begin selling drugs using the Internet, Zeglin said.

The most-organized criminal groups already are conducting some of their business on the Internet, according to Barry Glick, a psychologist who is on the Gang Advisory Committee for the Justice Department's Office of Juvenile Justice Delinquency Prevention.

Although Glick does not believe that they sell drugs directly over the Net, they have set up "systems for drug distribution, and they use the Internet and chat rooms for that," he said.

Law enforcement has little hard evidence of such activities because the gangs' methods are difficult to unravel. They can use innocuous keywords to refer to illicit goods and encrypt messages using programs available to any consumer. Experts are certain they employ "the same security functions you would have if you wanted to get into a Smith Barney account," Glick said.

Far more common, though, are the often crude home pages for neighborhood gangs. Their primary purpose is to create a sense of community among allies.

Laura Alviso, a 24-year-old junior studying creative writing at Eastern Washington University in Cheney, Wash., said she created her Web site for a "set" of Surenos known as Florencias. She wanted the site to be a tribute to her boyfriend, a Florencia who is serving time on a robbery conviction at Washington State Penitentiary in Walla Walla.

"There's a whole underground of these Web sites," she said. "Internet Web sites have become the place. It's like graffiti on the wall; there's graffiti on the Internet."

Alviso grew up among gang members in Washington's Yakima Valley, but she said she didn't respect the "cholos" until she realized "they do more than just hang around in the neighborhood and drink." Though she isn't a member herself, she has come to identify with gang culture and says her Florencia site is a matter of pride and brotherhood that transcends street rivalries.

She once complimented a gang Web master by the name of Scarface on the artistry of his home page for a branch of the rival 18th Street gang.

"I want to model my site after Scarface's," she said.

But old rivalries die hard. Alviso received a stinging message back from him: "Don't you get it? Florencias don't get along with 18th Streeters."

Unwitting Corporate Sponsors

Although there has been no bloodshed over this online strife, the gang sites have spawned some unexpected conflicts, including an embarrassing one with corporate America.

Gang members typically make their cyberhomes on sites operated by companies such as Angelfire, Homestead and Express Page, which offer free Web space and place ads on the sites to make money.

That arrangement has led several blue-chip firms to become unwitting financial sponsors of sites such as Crips.com, Sacramento Almighty Latin Kings Nation and others. Microsoft, Dell Computer and Best Buy have found their banner ads splashed across gang sites, along with such unlikely firms as ModernBride.com and Silicon Investor.

Companies such as Silicon Investor rely on marketing firms to distribute their ads around the Internet. Advertisers usually specify certain criteria to ensure that their ads reach their target audience, but it isn't a foolproof system.

"This doesn't sound like our typical Silicon Investor customer," quipped spokesman Steve Stratz upon learning that ads for the stock market Web site were placed atop a page for a Latin Kings gang. "I guess we're at least reaching a tech-savvy gang member."

Network Solutions, the company that manages the Internet's critical naming system, was so upset to learn that one of its ads had appeared on the site of a San Diego–based member of the Sureno gang that it had the site shut down.

But for the most part, gang sites are still only an obscure corner of the Web. The most notorious names in all of the gang world already have been taken—by a middle-age father of two in rural Cassville, Mo.

Dirk Lemmons isn't in any gang, but his roster of Web sites includes Crips.com, Bloods.com, Sureno.com, 18thSt.com and LatinKings.com. Not content with just a full complement of street gangs, Lemmons also owns Russian-Mafia.com, Mexicanmafia.com, Italian-Mafia.com and even Mobmusic.com.

Lemmons, 43, spent the early part of his career in a depressed area of St. Louis, where he said he roamed the streets with "a gun shoved down my waistband and a gun in my ankle." He sold security equipment such as iron window bars and managed apartment buildings in the highest-crime, most drug-infested areas of St. Louis.

All around him, he saw "very bright and intelligent kids that society had earmarked as worthless," he said. "I thought that at their age, they had the ability to turn their lives around."

So in 1998, he began building a series of gang intervention sites. Part of his strategy was to seize the most notorious names on the Web so they would not fall into the wrong hands.

"All we ask is that you [gang members] use this site as a place to get away from all the violence," reads a message on the Crips.com site.

After luring visitors, the site steers them to a "reality check" section that includes gruesome photos of murdered gang members, newspaper stories about victims of gang violence and e-mail from former gangbangers, including this poem:

> Little man all dressed in red.
> Where you think you going with that flag on your head?
> Came from a good mother why make her cry?
> Leave this house and you'll surly [sic] die.
> Just seen little man all dressed in blue.
> He looks like he wants revenge for something that doesn't even
>   involve you.

The Internet already has begun to swing Anthony, the Sacramento Web master, away from the streets. He devotes at least four hours a day to the SacTown Gangsta site, and now he doesn't have as much time to hang out with his friends.

Though he insists he is supporting himself just fine by selling CDs and other merchandise, he has begun to contemplate a real career in computer graphics. But the edginess in his voice makes it clear that he is worlds away from the dot-com life that lured so many talented young people to nearby Silicon Valley.

The messages left for him by 700 people who have visited his Web sites underscore the difference between his piece of cyberturf and the millions of more routine Internet outposts.

"Some people give me love," he said, "and some people say they want to kill me and find out where I live."

THE CHANGING LOOK OF GANGSTERS

Michael Krikorian

For many years, gang members have favored a certain look: baggy pants, football jerseys, bandannas, numerous tattoos. But as journalist Michael Krikorian points out in the following article, hard-core gangsters are beginning to realize that wearing this stereotypical outfit makes them extremely visible to the police. Instead, Krikorian explains, these gangsters are adopting a new conservative look of dress suits and ties, the better to blend in with conventional society and to help them expand into white-collar crimes. In an ironic twist, he notes, the hard-core gang members are abandoning their stereotypical wardrobe at the same time that the gangster look is gaining in popularity among young teens who are not involved in gangs. Krikorian is a staff writer for the *Los Angeles Times*.

These days gang members don't always look like thugs.

Taking advice from older criminals—some imprisoned, some retired but consulting, some still active—many hard-core gang members have traded their outfits for a more conservative look, a look police say enables them to expand into white-collar crimes without the early warning the old costume set off.

Abandoning Stereotypes

You may still have the classic Hollywood vision of a gang member: Baggy pants. Bandannas. Tattoos in full view.

But now a more conventionally dressed breed of gang member is emerging throughout Los Angeles. Some wear dress shirts and slacks, the better to blend in. And though not adopted by all gangs, the new look is proving to be a headache for law enforcement agencies as they try to keep track of the estimated 130,000 gang members in the county.

"It used to be we drive down the street and spot the gang members," says Lt. Gary Nanson, head of the Los Angeles Police Department Valley Bureau's Special Enforcement Unit. "Now they're less visible. You can't tell who the bad guys are."

Nanson and other investigators say the wardrobe change is linked to a recent move by gangs toward more sophisticated felonies, such as identity theft and credit card fraud.

"As far as credit card fraud, that is something we are finding more and more," said FBI Special Agent Steve Gomez, adding that even major Crip gangs—East Coast, Hoova, Rollin' 60s, Fo-Tray, Main Street, Eight Tray Gangsters—are involved.

A major fraud investigation is underway into one of those Crip sets. LAPD detectives said the case is so big that it was transferred to the financial crimes squad downtown.

"It's incredible," says James DeSarno, assistant director in charge of the FBI in Los Angeles. "They're not supposed to be doing that. They're supposed to be on the corner selling drugs."

Gangs Blend In

It's dinner time in Chinatown and LAPD gang expert Officer Jerry Velasquez is having a meal at the popular Ocean Seafood. He's irked to see gang members there savoring shrimp and lobster.

"This one guy was in a suit and he was reaching and his gang tattoo slipped out from his collar," Velasquez says. "But most people wouldn't know. You can be sitting at a nice restaurant and there's guys at the next table with suits and ties and they look like businessmen. But they're killers."

"Everyone's going 'low pro,'" says Gabriel Velasquez, a former member of Blythe Street, a Panorama City gang. "You got a lot of homies just be wearing regular clothes. Baggy pants is out of style now. Man, that was like letting the police know."

Not only do the police not know, neither does much of the public.

"People are always telling me they don't see as many gang members as they used to," says Nanson, who often addresses town hall meetings on gang awareness. "I tell them not to get a false sense of security. You actually need to be more cautious than before. They're just changing their look."

The police believe another reason for the wardrobe change is California's gang enhancement law, which adds years to prison sentences for crimes linked to gang membership.

Switching Wardrobes

In recent years, that baggy look has caught on with young people of all classes, most of whom aren't affiliated with any criminal gang. Even major clothing companies, such as Levi Strauss, have introduced lines of baggy jeans.

As a brilliant sunset bows out, a big teenager in a blazing red Jevon Kearse football jersey struts along Chase Street in Panorama City. If your profiling is out of date, this 16-year-old could be a poster boy for gang membership. Confident walk, black baggies, scarf almost completely covering his head and face. If he walked into a bank, they'd dive for cover.

But Robert Gudiel, walking home from his part-time job, is not a gang member. He just likes to dress this way.

"The police, they gotta update," Gudiel says. "They think I'm a gang member but the gangsters aren't dressing like this anymore. The police always stopping me and my friends. It kind of gets on your nerves after a while."

A few blocks away and a few hours later, on Willis Avenue, a stronghold of the Blythe Street gang, though there are lot of guys who look like the gang members of yesterday, none is. At least none claims to be.

Finally, three Blythe Street gang members pedal by on bikes. They swarm around a pretty young girl, then ride on.

Their hair is cut neat but not short, their pants and shirts fit well. They admit they are gangbangers but refuse to give their real names or street names because, as one puts it, "That be admitting, and with the new [gang enhancement law] thing, that be stupid."

"The old look, it was cool for a while, but now you gotta go low pro," says one of the teenagers who used to wear the clownishly sagging trousers that topped out at the lower buttocks and revealed underwear.

A Lethal Mistake

The popularity of the old gangster look can get an innocent killed. On May 5, 2001, Javier Hernandez was washing and waxing his cherished Chevy Suburban at his parents' home near Culver City.

He was wearing baggy shorts, had a shaved head and tattoos. He was not a gang member. In his 24 years, the only blemish on his record was one traffic ticket. But his look may have gotten him killed.

"Somebody may have thought he was a gang member," said Det. Mike DePasquale, homicide coordinator at LAPD's Pacific Division. "That's the only clue we have right now, the way he was dressed."

In part, the trend away from looking like a stereotypical gang member grows from prison and jailhouse wisdom, since inmates have plenty of time to figure out what went wrong.

"There a lot of gangsters dressing casually, like Miller's Outpost, like those malls, like, you know, like in long-sleeve dress shirts," says Fabian "Trigger" Nava, 34, a heavily tattooed former member of the Columbia Li'l Cycos clique of 18th Street.

He spoke by phone from the Wayside jail in Castaic, where he is trying to appeal a recent murder conviction. "Plus, everybody's shaving their head nowadays. You can't tell who's who."

Warned Lt. Nanson: "You're walking through the mall parking lot and you see some guys that look like gang members. Even if they're not, you avoid them," Lt. Nanson says. "Then you might walk right close past some nicely dressed guys and they might whisper 'Give up the Lexus.'"

HOMEGIRL SURVIVAL STORIES

Donna DeCesare

Donna DeCesare is a freelance reporter and photographer who has documented the rising tide of gang violence in the poor neighborhoods of Los Angeles. In the following essay, she interviews four girls who have survived the brutalities of gang life. As DeCesare reveals through these personal accounts, girls' motivational factors for joining a gang often arise from vulnerability rather than meanness, but they can be as ruthlessly violent as their male counterparts when goaded to revenge. On the other hand, the author notes, the responsibilities that come with young motherhood often force these girls to mature out of gang life much faster than the boys.

"Call me Angel," she says evenly, meeting my gaze. A faint scent of wet Pampers clings to her knit top after she places her toddler, Tonio, in blankets on the floor. Sinking heavily into a black Naugahyde couch, she begins. "It was supposed to be a kickback for us homegirls, a slumber party." I watch her "fangs"—those gravity-defying teased bangs favored by Latinas of a certain age—casting bird nest shadows on the mildew-stained wall as she speaks. Angel remembers waiting at the house with Dreamer while the other homegirls made a beer run. "There was a knock at the door. I got up thinking—'gotta be the homegirls,' but before I know what's up, my best friend Dreamer is yelling at me: 'Look, I'm the oldest, you get under the bed and stay there.' So I did it," Angel continues.

From her hiding place, heart pounding, eyes tightly shut, she could hear a familiar girl's voice screaming, "You bitch," then a blast of gunfire followed by a terrible silence. "I was thinking, 'Oh no, she's not dead. This ain't real,'" Angel trembles, rocking herself. "When I felt it was safe to come out, I found my best friend. You couldn't even see her face. You know, it was like they shooted her so much you couldn't even describe how she was."

When police arrived, Angel told them about the girl who'd been sending Dreamer messages on loose leaf paper with the number 187 written in blood. (A '187' is Los Angeles police code for a homicide; in gang parlance it's a death threat.) Angel hadn't glimpsed the mur-

Excerpted from "Avenging Angels: Homegirl Survival Stories," by Donna DeCesare, *Alicia Patterson Foundation Reporter*, 1999. Copyright © 1999 by the Alicia Patterson Foundation. Reprinted with permission.

derer's face, but she felt certain it was the same girl—a rival gang member who'd been jilted by one of her own homeboys and turned jealous when he began dating Dreamer. "My friend Dreamer kept saying she was going to die," she told the cops, sobbing. "I didn't believe her."

From Revenge to Regret

The cops on the case didn't believe Angel would make a credible witness. Unable to talk about her feelings with her angry and terrified mom or with anyone besides her homeboys, Angel came to a bitter conclusion: "The cops weren't going to make that girl pay for the murder of my best friend. The way I saw it, the only person who was going to make her pay—it was me. My homeboys were telling me: 'Don't do it. Let us do it. You're twelve. That's too young.' But I was like, 'No, that was my best friend. She's going to pay and I'm going to take her badge.'"

The conclusion of this story is grim, not unusual. Even as homicide rates have fallen nationally, the proportion of L.A. homicides that are gang related has doubled since 1980, now accounting for 40 per cent of all murders. That California's skyrocketing incarceration rates, which are now the nation's second highest, have had no apparent effect is especially alarming. Young Californians live in a state with 18 times as many gun stores as McDonalds restaurants—and in a nation with fewer federal safety regulations for guns than for teddy bears.

In the brutal world of L.A. gangs, youths view justice as a "do-it-yourself" project. Most of the mayhem occurs among teenagers over turf, status or revenge. Kids like Angel, from the housing projects, or kids from poor residential tracts, are growing up alone. They are neglected, feared or shunned by their fragmented communities and their own troubled parents. No one tried to stop Angel as she plotted the payback—no parent, no counselor, no teacher. Left to the company of her peers and the vigilante code of streets, where guns are readily available, Angel disguised herself as a boy and got away with murder.

Holding her head in her hands, nearly a decade later, Angel's voice grows quiet.

"Even though I did it in a good cause—killing her because she killed my best friend—It wasn't on me to let her pay for it. I should of let God take care of it." She looks up, wiping her tear-streaked face. "Now I think about that girl's mom or whoever was with her. I think about how they are. . . . I'm scared. I still have to deal with it every day of my life. When you take somebody's life you can't pay it. Even if you kill yourself, you can't pay it. It's not possible."

Seeking an Accurate Portrait of Girl Gangsters

Media outlets have recently developed a fascination with girl gangsters who kill. But this fascination has more to do with our society's fear of violent crime and its need to justify current crackdown policies, than with the realities of gang girls' lives, according to Dr. Meda Chesney-Lind, a sociologist who has been studying girls in the criminal justice system for more than 20 years. The fearsome image of marauding girls swelling the ranks of the 150,000 gun-toting gang members, roaming L.A. streets and shopping malls, ever ready to steal, kill and die for their gang, remains as ubiquitous as it is inaccurate. For Chesney-Lind, it amounts to a criminal version of the madonna/whore complex. "We either ignore women's violence entirely or we demonize it," she said.

Chesney-Lind admits that girls may be more numerous and that FBI data indicate a significant increase in the number of girls arrested for violent crimes. However, she argues such facts are largely irrelevant to the question of whether girls are becoming more violent. Chesney-Lind points out that FBI data show that roughly 10 per cent of youth arrested for violent crime are girls, and that this percentage has been constant for decades. Motivating factors for girls joining gangs are similar to those who become runaways or street kids. "It's still abuse, sexual abuse, and economic marginalization," she said.

Criminologists know that the criminal careers of most youthful offenders last only one year and that more than 80 per cent of those who commit a violent offense during adolescence mature out of such behavior by age 21. Girls age out of gangs faster than boys in part because of motherhood, according to Chesney-Lind. "Having a child forces you to change your relationships, expectations and responsibilities," she notes.

Chesney-Lind sees a selfishness in the baby boomer generation's policies toward youth. An assessment of youth oriented anti-crime programs conducted for the American Youth Policy Forum concludes that programs that provide individual attention from caring adults significantly reduce youth violence. "We know what kids need, yet we're dismantling family courts and trying juvenile offenders as adults. Girls face a society that is getting meaner," she said.

Most of the homegirls I met recently in L.A. seemed more vulnerable than mean. The tendency toward absolute judgment and vengeful remedies are hallmarks of adolescence that are enshrined in gang culture. But a combination of motherhood, maturation and supportive programs helped many of those I've talked with. Jessica Diaz, Mirna Solorzano and Herika Hernandez each followed a different path toward change.

Jessica's Story

I first met Jessica Diaz three years ago at the Ventura Training School, the only juvenile correctional facility in California that holds girls.

At fourteen, addled by an addiction to crack, she'd been persuaded to help her drug dealer rob a bank. "He said with the money, we could go away somewhere else. I hated my life. I wanted to escape as far away as I could," Jessica said, smiling at her foolhardiness.

As I learned more about her early life, such folly became understandable. From the window of their tiny house in El Salvador, three-year-old Jessica had watched as government soldiers took her father outside and shot him in the head. Years later in L.A., she and her brothers, Victor and Ulises, would run horrified as a gun battle with the Eighteenth Street gang mowed down their friends. That the three Diaz kids became Mara Salvatrucha gang members seems as unsurprising as the tragic fact that Jessica's brothers are now dead.

"I hated being locked up, but for me in a way it was like going away to college." Jessica said, remembering Ventura. She devoured books while she was there, thrillers, mysteries, romances. Her favorites were books by Sandra Cisneros and Luis Rodriguez—books about people like her. "I had a good psychology teacher who taught us parenting classes. It made me think a lot about me and my mom, about my family, and about how I wanted to raise my kids. I didn't want to keep repeating the same negative patterns over and over, you know. And damn, suddenly I could see it when I did something I didn't really want to do."

But parole, at first, was a road of rejection. Her son Carlos, born just before her arrest, had bonded with her mother during her absence and refused to accept Jessica as his mother. She found looking for work demoralizing and humiliating. "Not many people want to give ex-cons a job," she said, adding: "For a month I went back to the pipe . . . [crack]." But after locking her up for a few weeks to make a point, her parole officer helped her get a job at the Los Angeles Conservation Corp.

LACC is a visionary program that combines high school equivalency education and therapy with paid work on conservation or community improvement projects. For many former gang members, it creates a bond that replaces their gang ties as well as providing their first experience of work. Her nine months at LACC were the bridge Jessica needed.

Since LACC, Jessica has become a wife and a mother again. For the moment, she is content being a homemaker in the working class enclave of Huntington Park, bonding with her daughter, Cassandra, that she missed with her son. She and Danny would like Carlos to live with them, but Jessica recognizes that building a relationship will take time. Gazing at her son's photograph on the wall she said, "Carlos is all my mom has besides me, now that my brothers are gone. We can work it out."

Mirna's Story

At 7:00 A.M., Mirna Solorzano rises and prepares her son, Edwin, for their daily trek from South Central Los Angeles to L.A. Community College.

While Mirna sits in English Lit. class, Edwin attends a special kindergarten enrichment program on campus. When she can afford it, two-year-old Nathan stays with a babysitter. By half past seven, the babysitter still hasn't arrived. "We'd better go now," Mirna says, throwing one last nervous glance at the clock. She slings her book bag over one shoulder, cradles Nathan on her hip and reaches for Edwin's hand with her free hand, while closing the heavily grilled front door with her foot. The three will spend the next hour and a half snaking their way by bus through L.A.'s commuter traffic.

It's a short journey compared to the one Mirna has traveled to become a student again. Her childhood home life had the intensity of a political movement. Mirna's father was a trade union leader who'd fled death squads in El Salvador. From age five, when her family arrived in L.A., she went to political rallies. "My parents were fighting to be free, for El Salvador to be free and all that, but it got to such an extreme that I hated the guerrillas they supported. I felt, 'Why do I always have to be later on, later on,'" she said, gesturing her parents' presumed dismissal of her with her hands. "I wanted to go out, have fun."

The "cause" eventually strained her parents' fragile marriage. Mirna's mother began an affair with a family friend who years later became Mirna's stepfather. But when her mother was absent, the man made sexual advances. "I hated him and I hated my mother for believing him and not me," she said heatedly, remembering what happened when she tried to tell her mother about how he'd touched her. By fourteen, she was running away from home and attempting suicide.

Eighteenth Street gang crash pads became her refuge, and gangsters her guerilla fighters. "My homeboys tried to kill him once because of what he did to me," she said, referring to her stepfather.

It took a nervous breakdown and hospitalization at 18 to change Mirna's course. Mirna credits her therapist and social worker for the transformation that has sent her back to school, helped her begin a reconciliation with her mother, and to develop a respectful relationship with her father. A recent NPR radio report about Homies Unidos, a youth program which is helping gang members in El Salvador, caught her attention. "I'm going to contact them about starting something like that here in L.A." Squeezing her son Edwin's hand, she adds, "But I won't make the same mistake my parents made with me. My kids come before any program. I want them always to feel they can tell me the truth and can ask for what they need."

Herika's Story

At first glance, Herika Hernandez seems to have almost nothing in common with either Jessica Diaz or Mirna Solorzano except perhaps for her Salvadoran heritage. The poised tenth grader from Beverly Hills High has made honor roll consistently, was class president of her middle school and has her sights fixed on a career in law. But being so gifted can be a lonely experience for a teenager growing up in a housing project.

For years, Herika watched helplessly as her father humiliated and beat her mother when he came home in a drunken rage. Before her mother finally got the courage to leave, Herika began staying away from home. Her friends from school and the projects all had older brothers and sisters in gangs. By age eleven, Herika was wearing baggy pants and hanging with the Culver City gang. She knew that the gang would only bring trouble, but she was lonely, bored and desperate to escape tensions at home.

One of her teachers recognized what was happening and told her about the Fulfillment Fund mentoring program. The Fund is designed to help immigrant or poor kids of average or higher academic ability complete high school and set their sights on college. It makes a 10-year commitment to kids who join.

At first, Herika was worried about having a mentor. What could she talk about with someone so much older? But she liked Barbara Joy Laffy's warm humor immediately. With Barbara Joy, Herika has been able to explore a cultural world far away from the projects where she lives, without the accustomed alienation she feels at home. "I love classical music," Herika said after one of their outings. "It takes you places you've never been. My friends would think it's weird if I told them. Someday they'll understand."

Or perhaps not. Last spring, as Herika's fourteen-year-old brother and three friends walked home from school, a car of gang members drove up and began blasting at them. The boys ran into an alley but one boy was killed and another injured. "My brother's friend had just been jumped in [initiated into] the Culver City gang. The guys that shot were looking for him, but they killed another kid who wasn't in the gang," Herika recalled. Remembering how hard her mother took the news and the tensions it raised at home between her siblings, she added, "My mentor is like a second mother to me."

CAUGHT BETWEEN TWO CULTURES

Saroeum Phuong, as told to S. Beth Atkin

When he was seven years old, Saroeum Phuong and his family escaped the brutal Khmer Rouge regime in Cambodia. After several years in refugee camps, they settled in America, where Saroeum found himself caught between the traditions of his native land and the new culture that surrounded him. Feeling misunderstood and lonely, he sought solace in a local gang, the Boston Red Dragons. Although Saroeum gained a sense of identity in the gang, he also found trouble, becoming involved in robberies and fights. With the help of a persistent counselor who believed in him, Saroeum eventually left the gang and turned his life in a positive direction. Photojournalist S. Beth Atkin captures Saroeum's inspiring story in the following excerpt from her book *Voices from the Streets: Young Former Gang Members Tell Their Stories.*

We had a wonderful family when we first came to the U.S. We got here in August 1984—my four brothers, mother, father, and uncle. In November it started snowing. And my family had never seen snow. We went out and were throwing snowballs. The day my family arrived here was the best day of my life.

Escaping a Brutal Regime

We had no choice but to leave my country. There was war in Cambodia. There is a communist bullshit kind of thing. People were getting killed, and you didn't have food. It's like slavery. We had nothing over there. The Khmer Rouge thing, it was supposed to be a revolution to help the people. But instead it was to kill the people. People that have lighter skin get killed. My skin would be dead. And people who wear glasses, because that shows you are upper-class. And if you're in the Cambodian army, they kill your whole family.

My family was separated during the war. My brother Sarann, the oldest one, was forced to join the Khmer Rouge army to fight. I guess they killed a lot of people. That's what he told me. Like one day they had a festival, with good food and everything. The food was poisoned. He was able to escape. We lost him in 1975. Then in 1979 we

Excerpted from *Voices from the Streets: Young Former Gang Members Tell Their Stories*, by S. Beth Atkin (New York, NY: Little, Brown and Company, 1996). Copyright © 1996 by Little, Brown and Company. Reprinted with permission.

found him. We were losing all our connections. My father didn't know where my mom was, and she was pregnant. He didn't trust anybody at that time. He loved me a lot because I was the youngest. So he took me to the front line when I was about three or four years old. The Khmer Rouge was shooting at the Cambodian army he was in. I watched my father get shot. He blanked out 'cause he lost a lot of blood. So all I was doing was crying out and calling him. And then he finally got back up. And he said, "I'm dizzy." Now when I talk to him about the war, he tells me why he brought me with him. He says, "If I took you with me and thought you would be killed, then I have anger to fight."

I also saw these brothers who tried to run away from the Khmer Rouge camp. They caught them—let them sleep nice and smoke and eat before they kill them. They tied them up, their feet and their hands together, and put a rope through a tall coconut tree and lifted them up. Then they would drop them. The whole town was invited to watch. And when you see that, you don't scream, you don't cry, you don't feel, you don't think. They want you to laugh about it. They say people that are against Angka, they deserve to be tortured. Angka is like a god and the government of Pol Pot. Pol Pot was the leader of Khmer Rouge.

I left my country in 1979. We didn't come from Cambodia right to here. We were in two Thai camps. People were just running all over the place. It's a lot of confusion—the war and everything, the hunger. First at the camps, it was people building your own house and you grow your own things. But then it's like prison. The Thai government built a fence around the camp and had soldiers. I was there for about five years. Then we went to the Philippines, and we got here.

My parents and some older folks would not talk about what happened in Cambodia. They just keep it to themselves. That's why they get crazy. Our family didn't talk about it. I don't talk to anybody. My father don't talk to anybody. Everybody just shut their mouth. Before, we stuck together as a family. And when we came to this country, like damn, we're in the land of making a dream come true. And then it was like we split. I didn't understand it. I was a kid.

Difficulties in America

My mother worked two jobs when we came here. She worked really hard to get her family in the right place, trying to save some money for us to go to school. All she wanted was my father to stay home, go to school, and learn some English. And he doesn't do that. He's an alcoholic. I can't say nothing but the truth. He drinks a lot, and he likes to gamble. And I have two brothers who do, too. My father went out to get drunk and gamble and took all the money that my mother was trying to save. It was about forty thousand dollars, and he just wasted it in six months. We were supposed to buy a house. That must have been hell. Every penny earned was through her energy and sweat.

Just comes a time when a lot of things hit me at once. I got problems at home. My mother had it with my father. My parents don't get along with each other and filed for divorce. I didn't talk to anybody about the problems at home. It was an Asian traditional kind of thing. I asked my mom, "Why is everything this way?" And I remember clearly my mother said, "When you get older, you'll understand."

A lot of things are different over here. In Cambodia, we respect older people more than in this country. When we walk past them, we put ourselves lower. And in the Asian family, like I say, we don't communicate and you never attempt to show feelings. When you're parents, you don't say to your kid, "Son, I love you a lot. I hope you do good." I was waiting for my mom to say that for a long time. She tried, and I know deep inside of her she loves me and cares for me. But sometimes she doesn't show it. And Cambodian culture, it's not like the American family. I don't give my mom a kiss before I go to school or say, "How you doing, Mom?" We just go to school. The feeling never shows through to a son or daughter from their parents.

Also, nobody in my family really spoke English when we got here. So when I went to school, I didn't understand anything the teachers were telling me. I was dressed like a girl. But I didn't know it. I lived in East Boston, where the majority of people are Italian and white. And when I walked home, kids would swear at me, calling me names like "gook." Some of them were holding Christ in their lives and still called me gook. And they used to call me "you Chinese this and that." And I want to say to these people, "You're fucking stupid—I'm not even Chinese. So what does this have to do with me?"

Once these guys came up to me with hockey sticks. I was playing video games with the money I got for turning in cans. I was about fourteen, and they were about eighteen. They spit at me right in my face. I don't really say anything because I don't speak the language. So I keep playing and laughed with my friends, and this guy came over and smushed his cigarette in my favorite jacket and burned a hole, and I didn't have much clothes when I came here. The other guys smacked me in the head. So I tell my friend it's not worth it. And I walk home. I didn't tell my parents what was going on.

I couldn't explain it to my mom. If I told her they beat the shit out of me on the way home from school, she would tell me to shut up and I was a troublemaker. And then you have the people that speak English who don't understand you at school. Like you say, "I came from Cambodia," and they would say, "Where?" You have to point to the map. So in school they don't understand where I'm from. At home my mother don't understand what kind of situation I'm facing. If she did, she wasn't ready to deal with it.

That's when I started to hang out with guys in my neighborhood. It started out as a racial thing. You come to this country, people look at you differently. Treat you like dirt. It makes you feel hopeless. So now where do people turn? Like me, I turned to a gang. These guys grew up in the same place and had the same experience. I'm sure that they got called gook. We're all in the same boat. We weren't into alcohol; we didn't have guns. We were just kids hanging out. That's when I moved to Chelsea [a Boston suburb]. I was about fourteen or fifteen.

I felt like I got lost between two identities when I got involved in the gang. Your family rejects you when you join a gang. And then you go out on the street and society rejects you. You're living in American society, so you try to go with the flow. But in Cambodian culture, for example, you can't touch my head unless you're older than me. And if I go outside, people will say, "Hey, Saroeum," and tap my head. Sometimes it make you feel left out. You know, you say, Damn, they don't even respect my culture. And then when you go home, you bring the American society into the house, and then you get rejected there, too. When I came here, I didn't understand much about my culture or American culture. In a way, in the gang, we created our own culture.

It was totally different from gangs you've ever seen. I think the reason is, we weren't a gang because we wanted to be one—it just grew from a lot of love. It became a close family. Most of us have brothers in the gang. We would hardly take a beating from anybody. The reason is, if you were my brother, for example, and I see you get beat up, I'm not going to run. I'm going to go and help my brother.

And so the bond with the gang becomes stronger and, I guess, the identity with it. We were like ants. If something happens to one of us, we get in a group and try to find that person. And every time we walk on the street, people look at us weird. Basically, we grew up like one person. We were like a family, a government, a rule. Just a system for ourselves. We looked at the American people who were against our race. We have no clue what the hell they were doing to us. You don't play us out like that. We're going to tell you that we're here and we're staying. So we got to have some kind of a groundwork. I mean, I can't get a job. I can't do anything to get clean money. I can't sell drugs, because I'm not into drugs. So I have to do what we did. It's about, like, taking care of your family.

This time was difficult for my mother. She was there for me, but she was working hard and taking care of everyone. She's a good mother, but I think she was fed up with me. So she sent me down to live with my brother in Providence, Rhode Island. She didn't know he was into gangs. I went to school for one day down there and got kicked out. I lived in an apartment with fifteen other guys who all ended up in the gang. I was the youngest. There were three or four Asian gangs that came from California. We got in fights with them and with skinheads. It was for territory. We did different stuff, but we were not involved in drugs. Never. I think the reason is, for us, we used the gang as medicine. It's a positive energy in the bad. During those days we weren't breaking the law because that's how we took care of our friends.

Gang Life Becomes More Violent

Down there is when the whole activities changed and where we started the BRDs, Boston Red Dragons. Later, when we came back up to Boston, the police called us the Bloody Red Dragons. We would get together and talk about Cambodia on days when the sun would come out. We used Cambodian and American street language. Like someone in the gang, we call *poghma*, a close friend, or say, "What's up, homie?" Sometimes I feel, Damn, I never had a chance to meet those kind of people through a positive way. I wish I didn't have to go through the gang stuff in order to get to know them and find that love among ourselves. It's impossible to find that kind of love. We didn't mean to be negative, but sometimes society forced us to be.

It was because we had no money, no support, no nothing. These are kids who have no high school diploma and can't get a job. So we did a lot of house invasions for money and jewelry. The first one, I was at the front door by myself and four guys were at the back door. Two people had guns. I had a knife. I wasn't interested in a gun. I know it would help me at some point, but I know I have a really high temper. So I don't want to hold one. Nobody wanted to go to the front because they were scared. "OK," I say. "I'll go." I kicked the door and got hit with a baseball bat by the person inside. I was saying, Where are those motherfuckers? They finally break the back door and went in. We taped the people in the house, their mouths shut. We asked the guy who hit me, "Are you going to give us the money? Or we'll have to beat the shit out of you." And he said no. We pull his head up from the floor. One of my friends pulled out a gun and shot him through the earlobe. Then we got the money and got out of there. We would live on that money till there wasn't any, and then we would do it again. It freaked me out for a while. People think when you're in a gang, you can't feel anything, that you are just crazy young people running lost who are killing. Maniacs, like a cyclone. But there's a human young person. There's a human to me.

But during that time, there was no remorse. There was no time to say I'm sorry or to say forgive me. It was a time to survive. And that's when I was into the gang heavy. I was about seventeen. I came back to Boston. My street name was Tommy, for Tomahawk. I used to carry an ax with me. I didn't care if people knew I was in a gang. But if you messed with me, you knew. Around that time I could sometimes get work, like lifting trees. And I also started going back to school.

My mother paid for a private school, Cathedral High. I went in and out of school. There I got a reputation as a gang member. I dress in street clothes, and most of the Asians wore normal stuff. I would have a red tag hanging from my pocket. I got respect after I brought a gun to school. It's a stupid way, but it also helped with a conflict I had with some kids. Some of my teachers tried to understand me and get me to laugh. Some of school I really liked. I had a good friend there, and she introduced me to Molly.

I was in a lot of trouble when I met Molly. Having a lot of fights. I remember having a shootout with some other gang. During that time it was just downhill. My friend was going to the program Molly ran called ROCA [Reaching Out to Chelsea Adolescents]—it means "rock" in Spanish. It helps kids like me. She told Molly about me—that I painted and wrote poetry and that I was in a gang and in trouble. So Molly came to look for me. She just showed up on the basketball courts and introduced herself. She said, "Are you Saroeum Phoung? Do you have a street name you feel more comfortable to call you?" I told her she could call me Saroeum. So she tells me she did street out-reach. During that time my ear is deaf. I was, like, I don't give a fuck about ROCA. And I don't give a shit about her. You know, she's a white lady, and she doesn't know shit about me.

Building Trust

I didn't put my trust in her right away because there were other people that had tried to help me from other programs. But then she kept show-ing up while I'm on the street, drinking a forty. She would show up in the middle of the night. I mean, this lady used to call me at school to see if I was there. I had a beeper then, so she used to beep me, and she gave me all her numbers to call. I really hated her at this time. I felt like taking a gun and blowing her head off. I didn't see that she was helping me. One of the things that did help is that she persevered.

She didn't see me as a parent would, their kid drinking on the street. She was looking at my brain. I wasn't just a figure of me being on the street. I was a figure of a young person who has a lot of talent. So she kept open to me and was pretty good at handling stuff, like when I would shut down or attack her. I told her I was in a gang and that my life was pretty boring and I wanted to belong to it less. And suddenly she asked, "Are you able to talk to your family about this?" I told her that my family is not really organized and they're all screwed up. Except my mom. And she can't take care of everybody.

She gave me a ride and said, "You are talking about a lot of stuff which is good, and now I understand some of it." Then she asked me, "Saroeum, do you want to live or do you want to die?" And nobody had ever asked me that, and it's tricky and weird. I say everybody's born and they want to live. I don't want to die. If I wanted to die, I would have killed myself a long time ago. And after a while she said, "You're not about living, because you're about dying." She said, "You have the deci-sion and the answers inside of you. But you're afraid to put it out on the table and say that you're a man that can take care of yourself and that it's about a positive thing." And during that night, I was crying. It was so personal and touched me. I never had somebody to really listen to me. She said it's OK to cry. As a gang member I hardly see anybody cry. I told her, "Damn, I can't believe I'm crying in front of a white lady."

The next day I could see myself start to think about making a change. Yeah, in just one day. The whole day passed, and I figure we both don't remember anything about it. I went over to a friend's house for a party, and we were drinking and there were guns on the wall. Molly showed up again. She asked to be invited in to talk to me. She took me outside and asked if I thought about what we were saying last night. And I was like, yeah. And at those times I began to put trust on her. It was like being in my gang. If I have to rob a bank or do a home invasion for my gang, I would do that. And for Molly it's the same thing. She believes in young people making a change. She did this on her own time, on her own will.

She reminded me to call her anytime, and she tried to put me back in school. My mom paid for me to go to school, but they were ready to kick me out. Molly talked to them and helped me get back in. She kept telling me that she wasn't there to put pressure on me. She was there to help me make a decision. She brought me a choice.

Between my junior and senior year, I was arrested twice. One was for a racial fight. It was between an American and Asian kid. Between gook and gringo. They press charges on me, saying I cut somebody with a knife on the street. Molly came and helped to get the whole thing mediated. The charges were dropped both times. But I stayed in jail the second time for a week, and if you're absent from school that long, you flunk the whole quarter.

Newfound Success in School

So in my senior year I flunked two classes. The principal of my school said I couldn't graduate unless I made up the work and got a B and an A average. I had to study using a Kmai dictionary. I could learn to speak English on the street, but I would flunk if I had to write a test. Then I also read a lot of books about the Khmer Rouge. I ask a lot of people who were in and out of Cambodia. Because there is nothing in school about our culture. I talked to my history teacher and said every year there's a black history month and so I figure they should have a Cambodian month. Then she let me talk to my whole class. I told them where I lived and how we came here because of the war. I showed the video *The Killing Fields*. And now they know on the map where my country is and could understand where I came from. They don't look at me that I'm just another Asian guy. We're Asian but, you know, Chinese, Vietnamese, we all have different experiences.

So instead of hanging out, I would read a lot. I wrote a lot of poetry, too. And I would do painting, mostly landscapes and sunsets of my country. It was peaceful, like meditation, and put me in a good mood. So when I came home, I had a lot of energy to do work. I did a big painting and I was surprised how good l was. I felt good about it. The teacher thought I could go to art school someday. I worked really hard during that time. It was a tough year to finish school, but I showed I could make it.

When I graduated, Molly was there. My parents didn't come. I guess at that time they didn't care. If it had been my son, I would be damn sure to be there unless I was in prison. I was pretty mad, and I wasn't going to go. But Molly said they must have had something to do. And when I got up to get my diploma, everybody got up and said, "Gang member." It was a positive kind of thing. I guess they were proud of me somehow. I was all ready to cry. I said to my professor, I have it, I have it! I was like, damn, I accomplished something.

Giving Back to the Community

I was going to ROCA while I was finishing school, and after school I started to work there. It's a multiracial kind of place. The kids are involved running it, not just adults. I do street outreach near schools and talk to kids and see what's up. I also teach volleyball and kick boxing. My father taught me Cambodian kick boxing. I teach a more American kind of kick boxing, not as dangerous. It's good to teach kids self-defense. When I teach, I also talk to the kids. I find out if they show up at school. I tell them don't drink, don't smoke, and if they have family problems and can't talk to anybody, to come and talk to me. And we do.

I was a junior when I met Elizabeth, my wife, at school. She also worked at ROCA. She had problems, too, but she still was with me. She's Cambodian but was never in a gang or anything. She's a tough lady even though she's quiet most of the time. And you know, she would buy me books, pencil, pens for my study. Elizabeth and I, we went through everything together. Now we have a son.

His name is Sombatchey, and he is almost two. When Elizabeth was pregnant, my friends told me to go to a good American doctor for an abortion because I couldn't take care of him. I proved them wrong. And I guess the kid really pulled me out from the street. I was feeling like any fool can make a baby, but it takes a real man to raise a child. I'm lucky to be his dad. . . .

I tell Molly a lot and Elizabeth, too, I want to go to college and start writing. And the message, if I was going to write my own book, is that you don't have to be Asian to face this kind of problem with gangs. You don't have to be black, or white, or Latino. It could be anybody who can relate to the story I'm telling. I would want to get across there is always a choice for people who are involved in a gang. Don't wait until it's too, too deep. Like kill twenty people and go to jail and never get out. Wake up and think about yourself and where the hell you are at right now. See people like Molly inspire people like me. And it takes—what is the word? It takes a whole village to raise one child. It's true. I'm that one kid.

CHAPTER 4

THE CAUSES OF GANG INVOLVEMENT

Gang Membership Can Fulfill Many Adolescent Needs

Francine Hallcom

In 1996, Francine Hallcom, a professor at California State University in Northridge, began a long-term study of the Latino street gangs of Los Angeles and Ventura counties in Southern California. Hallcom has interviewed over 1200 young people in her ongoing study in an effort to understand the socio-economic experiences that lead youths to join gangs. In the following essay, Hallcom notes that all adolescents have specific needs, such as emotional support, prestige among their peers, and spending money. Inner-city teens who are immersed in poverty and receive little positive feedback from family members are often drawn to gangs as the only resource that fulfills many of these important needs, she suggests.

In the last few years, law-enforcement and public schools everywhere have experienced a virtual epidemic of youth violence that is rapidly spreading from the inner cities to the suburbs.

Gang tumult has become a nationwide catastrophe not only in the country's large metropolitan centers, but in the small urban and rural areas as well.

Gang activity not only means unsightly graffiti, but accelerated crime and dropout rates, the deterioration of neighborhoods, parks, and playgrounds, and wasted human resources everywhere. Gangs are no longer just the problem of those who live in the crime-ridden neighborhoods where the gangs thrive; they are now everyone's problem.

Los Angeles is regarded as the nation's gang violence capital. And an important first step toward solutions that work is understanding the forces that cause youths to join gangs.

The research conducted in this study focuses on Los Angeles and Ventura County's lower-socioeconomic neighborhoods, the typical Wilsonian "destructive environment [as described by researcher William Wilson]."

Most of the literature reviewed here is limited to Latino gang members, male and female, and to nongang-affiliated youth from the same barrios. African-American and Asian gangs are undeniably prevalent in the same and near-by areas. However, the scope of any investigation must have parameters.

Additionally, Latino youths, whether first or fourth generation, are swayed in one way or another by a different culture, one that functions unlike the other two in its philosophy and general ties to family. Therefore, there are definite aspects of Hispanic street gangs that distinguish the members from their African-American and Asian counterparts. . . .

The Gang's System of Rewards

According to social learning theory, individuals acquire certain behaviors and attitudes via a process of social learning—in this case from gang peers and delinquency. Social learning theory claims that if behavior is rewarded and repeated episodes are met with reinforcement, it continues. Of course, if behavior is punished, the perpetrator is discouraged from engaging in the conduct and the behavior decreases. Hence, the notion—gangs facilitate instrumental conditioning.

Certainly, if there are no interested parents to step in with moral and ethical values of their own at this point, a potential recruit learns through close interactions with the gang members what is "appropriate or inappropriate," at least according to their reverse value system.

Actually, for many years research has pointed out that the gang merely speaks to most adolescent needs; that is, the need for affiliation, belonging, and for status or at least estimation. Gangs provide the necessary audience for deeds of bravado and for positioning and strutting. The gang fulfills a number of not-so bizarre needs after all; it provides a sense of family and of group membership by furnishing friends and camaraderie to unloved and often unwanted youngsters.

In this milieu with its own system of rewards, even though many realize that education could provide upward mobility, harsh socio-economic reality does not advance education as a realistic option unless there are parents or extended family members who promote hard work and striving as a value.

Instead, the immediate surroundings (and often even wayward parents) say to the youngster, "You're going nowhere from here." Or, as Veto put it, "My step-father always said I would end up in prison." Not a very nourishing or encouraging climate for a boy like Veto!

Some young people in the neighborhoods are genuinely afraid of becoming victims of gangs. Some join for the protection the gang gives them. Standard gang methods of intimidation range from extorting lunch money to physical beatings. The current investigation concurs. Two boys said they were tired of being assaulted:

Veto: "Finally, I said—Man, if you can't beat 'em. Join em."

Interviewer: "So you joined to get away from all the hassles?"

Alex: "No hombre—dile la verdad (No, man—tell the truth)—He was going with the tirachas too (dating African-American girls)."

Interviewer: "So that's why they were giving you a hard time?"

Veto: "Yeah—but there was lots of things. One time these two dudes jumped me on the way home from school for no reason. I was 10 years old—the f - - - - - broke my nose—see here. (Pointing to a ridge on his nose) Orale! That was ugly."

Alex: (laughed the whole time Veto told his story)

Veto: "He was one of them (pointing to Alex). Finally when I was about 16 I started going to things with them—you know? I don't like pain esa! Do you like pain?"

Interviewer: "What other reasons did you have—come on. Why else did you join?"

Veto: "You know—it all just happens. One day you're in. It's not like I planned it—sabes (you know)? Pero si (I tell you)—estos cabrones siempre estavan detras de me al chingaso." (Peppered with cursing, the translation is something like, "These jerks were always after me with their fists.")

Thus, the profile of the youth who joins might include the following: a youth with low self-esteem and a stressful home life. A youth who is friends with gang-members and experiences peer-pressure to join. A youth with poor academic performance, lack of alternatives, lack of positive support, feelings of helplessness, and hopelessness, as well as a very frightened youth who is intimidated by the gang.

The Lure of Easy Money

Gilbert: "I was a good student until junior high. I always did my homework and all that. But still I was behind. I could tell. My cousins went to (name of school—a parochial school nearby) and they knew more than I did. We would go visit them on Sunday sometimes and I could see that I wasn't going anywhere with school. They didn't teach us nothing."

Interviewer: "So why did you drop out?"

Gilbert: "I got a job. I got tired of never having any money—not even a dime! You wouldn't believe it. I didn't have no money—and I got fed up with that and I went to work."

Interviewer: "How old were you?"

Gilbert: "Twelve."

Interviewer: "What kind of job could you get at twelve? Who hired you?"

Carlos: "You could say he went into sales." (gales of laughter—Carlos bent over and did some hand signs)

Gilbert: "Yeah, sales and distribution." (more laughter)

In addition to an underground economy for the jobless, a gang extends club membership and belonging as described. . . . Both are powerful incentives to join.

Of course, a number of individuals sell drugs outside of and completely apart from the structure of the gang—as private peddlers, so to speak. Others have subgroups with whom they deal, usually the same individuals over and over again, ever suspicious that a new buyer is a "narc." Almost all the gang-affiliated participants in the current sample reported having sold drugs at some time or other whether in large or small quantities.

The Importance of Family Bonds

However, before one feels too sorry for Gilbert, it is important to remember that there are young people in the very next apartment living on the same street in the same type of environment who do not join gangs, who do not sell drugs, who also get beaten up, but who rise out of these environments triumphant. What appears to make the difference? The pattern that emerged in the current research is having a parent, or parents, a grandmother, uncle, brother, or other family member who is supportive and with whom the youth has such a bond that s/he would do nothing that would seriously jeopardize that relationship.

It appears that for youths in poverty-ridden areas, success in education soon becomes a fraudulent aspiration. As a result, getting a decent job, a high-paying job, is also untenable. Then, too, because of the poor job market in economically disadvantaged areas, for minority youth there is no real "future." Many who did not affiliate "settled" as one individual put it, but these young people repeatedly had bonds with someone they chose not to disappoint at any cost.

Tony: "I took a job—at a super market. I knew it didn't have no future—like getting raises or promotions, but I just took it to have money. I settled for that for now anyway, and started right away trying to find out what other people at the store were into. Stuff like that. I knew I couldn't just stay here—I come and see my Mom and my family and like that, but I don't hang out very much. I work overtime and all the time. Hell, I don't even want to be here right now. I'm just coming to see my Mom and my abuelo (grandfather)—just visiting. It's like a cancer here. You can get any kind of drug or weapon you want around here."

Tony was working in a super market in a neighborhood not far away that he perceived as less gang-ridden than the one in which his mother and her wheelchair-bound grandfather lived. Although he did not see his current employment as a career, he had settled for it even though he reportedly was experiencing many financial hardships. The present job was a passport out of his neighborhood. Tony was just visiting at the time of the interview.

The need for money is clearly a driving force for youths like Tony as well as for those who opt to join gangs or sell drugs. Money from drugs is not administered by the gang as an entity. Actually, money from drugs gives individual members status. If such monies are in any way pumped back into the gang, it is via highly indirect avenues. For example, individual or group monies obtained from drug sales were not used for what might be called "gang equipment;" i.e., guns, cars, crash pads, etc. Instead, money of any kind was spent on partying—providing food, beer, rides, gasoline, etc. Most members use the money they acquire for personal matters—to buy clothes and other goods. Some use drug sales revenue to buy things for their kids. . . .

In trying to uncover the reasons why some youths join gangs and others do not, there is a passing parade of unfulfilled needs to which the gang responds admirably. Reputation repeatedly came up in the interviews. It seemed to take on exaggerated proportions. The entire notion of status and reputation was utterly exaggerated and out of sinc with the rest of the world. The young men more so than the young women expressed a need to maintain an image; they were at times excessively needy in this respect, yearning to be important and craving recognition as fervently as a star-struck youngster coveting fame and celebrity. Of course, being in a gang causes others to fear them, and in their reversed value system, striking fear in the hearts of others gives status and prestige thereby bolstering their reputations.

Consequently, to insult a member via signs, trespassing onto turf, or any other seemingly inconsequential transgression, is to insult reputation with all the significance it carries. These little infractions become an affront not only to the individual, but to the entire group. To the rational mind, the violence with which gangs often react to many of the seemingly trivial transgressions is inexplicable.

According to researchers David Berland, John Homlish, and Mark Blotcky, "Psychologically, gang membership occurs during the developmental phases between childhood and adulthood, when disruption is common in respect to self-identity, establishment of trustworthy relationships, and determination of vocational choice."

In the surveys, a number of gang-affiliated adolescents report having been fairly good kids throughout grades K through 6. They also reported a surprising number of positive experiences in school as well as good feelings toward a number of their teachers.

However, at this crucial point, somewhere between grades 6, 7, and 8—between childhood and adulthood—many grow weary of the harsh living conditions that surround them, of never having any spendable cash on hand, and of waiting for love and reward from remiss parents. In the interviews, many said it was around junior high that they joined, or first began keeping close company with the gang. In the current study, this pattern appears to emerge again and again.

Gang activities entice many youths. Drinking, drug use, creating disorder, and vandalizing property are all seen as fun. Partying, getting high, bullying people, and robbing designated targets are just part of the merriment and amusement.

It is important, though difficult, to remember that the youths themselves, including some of the nongang-affiliated, did not consider the gang to be altogether deviant. Many gang- as well as nongang-affiliated also perceived the gang as a source of love and respect for those who become members. Even the nongang-affiliated said that those who join do so because, "It's like a family." This statement was made repeatedly in the interviews. On the street, they greet each other with signs, slaps on the back, secret hand-shakes, and quite often with embraces!

Good Apples and Bad Apples

There were sometimes siblings who joined and others who did not. Irrefutably growing up in the same household does not insure the same up-bringing for each child no matter how much parents may think so.

In the current investigation, families very obviously had preferred children even though they vehemently claimed to deal with each child in the same way. Sometimes the eldest children had special privileges. Sometimes they had a tremendous burden of chores and responsibilities. Sometimes the baby was spoiled and pampered (and became the gang member). In other families the baby virtually grew up on his/her own—utterly unattended. Some families appeared to have whipping boys, or "bad apples." By virtue of nothing more than the label in itself, this individual was treated differently. Therefore, this particular child was growing up in an environment unlike that of his/her siblings (the good apples) even though they were all living under the same roof. Of course, these are merely parenting topics and strategies known to the more educated members of our society, but unknown to most of the parents in impoverished neighborhoods.

For example, in the case of "Lolo," a gang-affiliated boy, there are three other brothers in the family, none of whom are gang members. Lolo's parents did not understand why there had to be one "bad apple" in the bunch. Both parents were interviewed; both were hard-working, cordial, and warm human beings. According to Lolo's mother, the boys were all treated and loved equally. According to Lolo, however, he was always picked on, teased, and humiliated by the others who went unpunished for their behavior. Lolo expressed a great deal of resentment and hostility toward his mother and brothers. It is probable that as he got older, he acted out more than the others, and was therefore punished more than the others in an ever-escalating vicious circle. There were no other family members—aunts, grandmother, etc.—for whom he had any regard. Lolo claims he was always taunted by all of them.

Lolo: "I was always the f—— -up. Everyone said I was no good ever since I was a little chavalito (kid). Now, they don't say anything to me anymore. Nobody messes with me."

Lolo's girlfriend tended to confirm most of his examples, arguing with only one or two minor points. She added that his family wouldn't dare say anything to him now! This, of course, was spoken in adulation. . . .

Something else that needs to be considered is ethnic identity, which more often than not is unquestionably negative in both Los Angeles and Ventura Counties where anti-Mexican sentiment abounds.

Researcher Shirley Brice Heath tells us that the self-concept of inner city youths is plaited with ethnic identity and gender. How a youth like "Lolo" develops a bad attitude is indeed complex: Brice-Heath claims young people's identities are multilayered self-conceptions that represent far more than simple labels of ethnic or racial membership. Add to that the disparaging view of the society at large, the labels, seemingly harmless—"pendejo" (coward), "stupido"—that Lolo was called as a child, and self-concept clearly is undermined. Gangs are almost always expressions of social disaffection—the politics of intransigence.

Friendships

In these communities, car cruising and low-riding have become a way of life. The car culture, which is subscribed to by both gang- and many nongang-affiliated youths, also serves as a rite of passage. The very act of driving a car with a few friends symbolizes adulthood and even rugged manliness. To see and be seen makes every day a veritable parade.

Other rites of passage exist as well. Some spoke briefly of an initiation, but most would not elaborate. Some youths claim they did not have to give up nongang friends, and said they have remained on friendly terms with neighborhood pals as part of loyalty to the "hood" or "el barrio."

However, according to other literature gangs do not encourage members to have friends, especially close friends, outside the gang. In the current investigation, although members repeatedly claimed they could run around with anyone they wanted, the nongang-affiliated tended to distance themselves from long-time friends once those individuals became gang members. In addition, the gang members tended to prefer their gang friends to their former buddies who were nongang-affiliated.

However, it might well be that the greater the proportion of gang-affiliated friends an individual accrues, the greater the social forces sucking that person into the gang and into more and more gang activity.

This whole issue becomes particularly important for those who work in intervention and prevention programs. Can the nongang-affiliated be useful in pulling at-risk or even inducted gang members out and away from the gang? Or should we keep the nongang-affiliated as far away as possible from those on the edge?

Teens are also bombarded with MTV music videos, concerts and other programs glamorizing and promoting "bad boy entertainment," "East Coast/West Coast rap feuding," and the violence perpetrated by the drug culture and street gangs. Back-to-school sales gimmicks promote the drudgery of school itself and the fun of buying new clothes. There is never a word about the joy of learning—nothing about securing a solid education, nothing about upward mobility through education!

If there is any hope, it may be in the pattern that emerges here; that consistently in this study the teens who thought highly of their parents or other extended family member(s) were those who were nongang-affiliated and who planned to stay in school. More recent research considers a dearth of parental or teacher role models good predictors of gang membership.

The exception here is a group of young men categorized as "Mama's Little Darlings."

"Mama's Little Darlings" are young men many of whom became gang-affiliated even though they enjoy strong relationships with their mothers. However, they were individuals who evidently received no discipline or clear-cut parameters from these ladies. The mothers were supportive of anything their boys did (there were no girls in this category, nor time within the scope of this study to inquire thoroughly into such a category for females). These mothers even blamed the police for harassing their little darling who was only smoking a little marijuana or snorting a little coke. A "boys will be boys" attitude pervaded most of these mothers' outlooks concerning their sons no matter how serious the charges.

The Need to Belong

In the barrio, traditions of unity and group run deep. Internally discrimination in the barrio, Latino against Latino, lies in loyalty to country of origin; thus, Mexicans are sometimes not fond of Guatemalans, who are not fond of Honduranians, who think Colombians are conceited, and on and on. Even second and third generations are frequently afflicted with this malaise. Add to this the rejection experienced by most Latinos from the predominant culture and it becomes a bit easier to conceptualize the compelling inner need for acceptance expressed by so many Latino youths. Among gang members, it is a need that some profess even in their dying breath. The need to belong also translates into the need to tell others where s/he is from—ergo the signs, the colors, the tattoos.

Partying and "getting down" with the others is an integral part of gang life, which in turn offers members many social contacts that may not have been previously available. Loyalty outweighs personal interests. An individual cannot merely assimilate into the gang without proving worth to the group. Members see themselves as security guards protecting turf in an ongoing feud with rival gangs, police, or anyone else who threatens them. The gang comes first and is the most important part of a member's life.

DIRECTIONLESS TEENS ARE VULNERABLE TO GANG RECRUITMENT

Steven L. Sachs

For many teenagers, the daily routine of school, chores, family responsibilities, and homework can become extremely boring, especially if they lack a firm sense of direction in their life. According to youth counselor Steven L. Sachs, these young people often view the world of gangs as being full of adventure, danger, and excitement. Gangs' distinctive monikers, hand signs, clothing, and jewelry can offer impressionable teenagers an instant sense of identity and confidence, he asserts. In the following excerpt from his book *Street Gang Awareness: A Resource Guide for Parents and Professionals,* Sachs explains how gangs subtly employ their allure to recruit vulnerable youths.

Teenagers look at their parents and see their lives as humdrum and boring. Parents get up, go to work, pay bills, watch TV, go to bed, then repeat the process day in and day out. Except for a few outside activities—weekend chores, shopping, visits to friends, family outings—adult life appears pretty sedate. For a bored teenager, the lure of the gang is a powerful one. It promises adventure, intrigue, danger, a sense of the unknown—hunting down rival gang members while being hunted oneself.

But, in truth, being in a gang can also be boring. Gang members who don't go to school tend to sleep in late, sometimes until the afternoon. They get up, drink a pop, play a video game, then go out and "hang" with their homeboys, talking, bragging, and lying about past exploits, crimes, fights, and anything else that happens to be the current topic.

Gang Life Is Enticing

As day gives way to night, gang activity steps up. Parties, drive-by shootings, city lights, cops and robbers, hanging out—let the gang banging begin. The adrenaline rush gang members were after all along finally begins to flow. The fringe members don their gang jewelry and clothes, which was not permitted in school, and join the evening's gang activities.

Kids get a sense of identity and recognition from being in a gang. It sets them apart from their classmates and family; they achieve status among their peers. This is especially important if they are unable to succeed in other ways, such as through school, sports, or employment.

Kids get a sense of power by being in a gang. Alone, these youths feel small, powerless, inadequate. They lack direction. Belonging to a gang, however, makes them feel powerful, invincible. They have direction at last—the direction of the gang—and they finally feel a sense of belonging. This need for direction and belonging leaves kids vulnerable to the recruitment tactics of gangs.

Gang Recruitment Methods

Gangs recruit new members in many ways. While some intimidation still goes on, this seems to have given way to subtler methods. For example, gang members will describe all the good things gang life offers: money, friends, parties. Gone are the days when you could go down to the local department store and bring home a pair of Keds, Red Ball Jets, or Converse All Star sneakers for less than $15. Today's high-tech athletic footwear, sports team Starter jackets, and ten-karat gold jewelry cost a good sum of money. We're talking about a serious cash-flow problem. When known gang members go around flashing wads of bills, wearing gold jewelry, and dressing in designer sports apparel, gang life may seem too good to pass up. Gangs can bring immediate gratification to an economically disadvantaged youth. This can be a big draw, particularly in areas where jobs are low-paying or scarce. According to recent reports, the economic advantages to gang membership are so attractive that older males have begun to join. Their cash flow, of course, comes from less than honorable means—drug sales, gun running, extortion, robbery, burglary, and theft.

At first, with the promise of fortune dangling before them, many younger gang members unwittingly become pawns to the older members and are forced to carry out illegal activities. The older members know that if they commit the crimes themselves and are caught, they will certainly face jail terms, whereas younger members receive lighter sentences like probation and informal supervision. But time is rarely on the side of these young gang members. Just as they begin to see the gang's economic and hierarchical inequality, it's often too late. They find themselves on the way to juvenile prison.

At school, gang members recruit kids in more subtle ways. Members who attend school—and there are surprisingly many who do—are always on the lookout for kids who are picked on or shunned by other classmates. They befriend these kids, making them feel safe and accepted. Vulnerable kids see protection in a gang. There is power in numbers; if once they were picked on, now they are surrounded by dozens of gang members ready to back them up. For kids today, this backup, a cadre of instant friends, is one of the most appealing rewards of being in a gang.

A Sense of Family

When asked why they have joined a gang, many members reply that they feel like part of a family. In fact, gangs use this in their recruitment pitch: There is another family waiting for you—all you have to do is join. This pitch particularly appeals to children from single-parent families.

Actor and director Edward James Olmos directed and starred in the powerful major motion-picture about gang life, *American Me*. In conjunction with the film, he also produced, directed, and narrated an excellent anti-gang documentary called *Lives in Hazard*, using current and former gang members who received small acting parts in the movie. The title of his documentary refers to Big Hazard, the name of a gang in east Los Angeles.

In the film, Timmy, a member of Big Hazard, drives home a very important message:

> When I needed someone to play ball with, someone to play catch with, I always had older homeboys like Moon Dog, Flappers, . . . and them. They were around, and they were there for the kids, and they'd throw the baseball with me for an hour, half hour, even if it was five, ten minutes. Ya see, they became role models in my life. I didn't look at them as gang members. I didn't look at them as a bad person. I looked at them as somebody that paid attention to me.

This reasoning would come as no surprise to former gang member Nicky Cruz, now a minister working within his own outreach program in Colorado. During the writing of his book, *Code Blue*, Cruz telephoned police working with gang units in large cities and small towns across the nation to ask what they thought was the number one reason kids join gangs. Every police officer gave the same answer: the breakdown of the family. In many cases, Cruz reports, there is no positive male role model in single-parent homes. A youth at risk will often identify with the nearest male. Unfortunately, that particular male may be involved with gangs or drugs. Even when both parents reside in the home, supervision and interaction may be inadequate, especially if both parents work outside the home. Also, if the parents themselves are involved with drugs or crime, or are verbally or physically abusive, the child may find friends with a similar background. The need for family, for those who love and accept us, is a powerful human need. Either we as parents supply it for our children, or the gangs will.

Recruitment is also influenced by a child's environment. If a child lives in a gang-infested neighborhood, he or she is expected to join a gang. This is where threats and intimidation play an important role. These children are motivated by fear. Many join to avoid harassment from neighborhood gangs, or to protect themselves against outside rival gangs corning into the area. Rival gangs entering a neighborhood frequently mistake innocent kids for gang members. Either way, these children are in danger.

Family environment plays an especially important role in the recruitment process, particularly when relatives themselves are in a gang. Among Hispanic gangs, it is not unusual for generations of family members to belong to the same gang—a family tradition, if you will. African American gangs, too, have shown a marked increase in second-generation gang members in the last decade. When a child is raised by a parent who is a gang member, the gang lifestyle is taught to and lived out in front of that child at a very early age.

Gradual Involvement

Recruitment can also take place through gradual involvement in social events. Prospects, or non-gang members, are invited to parties where they may be given free drugs, booze, even sex. Of course, prospects must eventually "pay up" for all the free entertainment. Sometimes they find themselves wishing to continue that lifestyle. Either way, gang recruiters have their victims right where they want them—hooked.

Less insidious but no less dangerous are gang members who allow children to just hang out with them, acting tough. Even without full-blown membership, these kids experience their first sense of belonging and respect. The unspoken deal is this: If you want to be cool and hang with us, then you need to join us.

ADULT ABSENCE CAN LEAD TEENS TO JOIN GANGS

Mike Clements

In the following selection, Mike Clements discusses the crucial role that parents play in determining whether their children will be attracted to gangs. Parents who are both loving and strict, who are involved with their children, and who create a secure home minimize the likelihood that their teens will join gangs, Clements writes. On the other hand, he contends, when parents are emotionally absent, overly lenient, or unable to provide a stable home life, their children become more susceptible to the security that gangs appear to offer. The author illustrates his message through a vivid account of the experiences of a young woman who rebelled against her uncaring mother by joining a gang. Clements is a reporter for the *News Herald* in Panama City, Florida.

Many people are looking for ways to answers to society's gang problem. Some believe law enforcement is the solution. Some believe education is the key. But one former gang member says the remedy can be found in only one place: at home. Too many gang members never had one, she says, not a home with parents loving enough to be there and, when necessary, be strict.

Actually, "former gang member" is something of a misnomer. The young mother who talked about her experiences as a gang member said that if it wasn't for the benevolence of her former gang leader, she would spend her days looking over her shoulder as she looked after her baby.

That leader liked her and allowed her to leave the gang's territory. Though he knows where she is, he has agreed not to bother her, so she can get on with her life.

Absent Parents Breed Resentment

Looking back, "Kim"(not her real name) said the reason she joined a gang is at once complex and simple. Summing it up in one sentence, she makes a statement that most teen-agers mutter from time to time.

"I just didn't like my mom," she said.

Kim's gang odyssey actually began in a small town in another state. As a baby she was abandoned by her mother and reared by an alcoholic father. When her father was put in prison, her mother suddenly reappeared, asserted her parental rights and moved Kim to another state.

The 13-year-old resented the woman she had never known, resented being forced to uproot her already turbulent life yet one more time and resented the fact that she had no say in the matter.

"It was really a blowup for me," she said.

Looking for ways to rebel, Kim began running with a rough crowd. Her mother seemed powerless, or unwilling, to take charge of her wild young daughter, and Kim continued to push the limits.

The Lure of the Gang

One night at a party, she got into an argument with another girl. The girl began to flash hand signs as they argued. A boy at the party realized that Kim didn't know what was happening and—in a move that was both merciful and malevolent—intervened before the matter came to blows.

The boy explained to Kim that her adversary was flashing gang signs, alerting other gang members to the trouble that was about to start. He explained how gang membership could benefit her and told her how to join.

He was doing more than providing information. As a high-ranking gang member, he felt Kim was a good candidate for recruitment. According to Kim, he was correct in his assessment.

When Kim joined the gang, she was given the option of having sex with every male member of the gang, or fighting five of the males for five minutes each. She decided to fight.

"It's pretty low to sleep with that many people," she said.

Her decision marked her physically—she still carries scars from the initiation—and socially. Because she chose to fight her way into the gang, she was seen as a person to be reckoned with. As she walked the halls of her school, Kim said other students deferred to her because word of her exploits had spread.

"I fought back and I never cried or complained about it," she said. "They knew what I was about."

The gang offered her protection from those who didn't take the stories seriously. Some kids wanted to challenge her. But even if they were bigger and stronger, they learned quickly that fighting her meant fighting the entire gang.

"It was like having security around me 24/7," she said.

But that security came at a price. Gang membership meant doing the bidding of gang leaders. The gang that Kim belonged to dealt drugs, burglarized cars and was involved in robberies. In addition to the typical street crimes associated with gangs, the teen-agers Kim hung out with adopted some old-style techniques for shoplifting.

For years, crooks have used diversions in public places to commit crimes. Kim said the gang was no different. She said they would often stage fights or disturbances in stores. Two gang members would engage in a mock argument, and one member who had a pacemaker would even fake a heart attack, to distract store personnel.

While store employees dealt with the phony situation, other gang members would take shoes, clothing or whatever they had come for.

"We took whatever we could and we were gone," she said.

More than once Kim's fighting skills were called upon to help settle a score with a rival gang. Rivals were beaten and intimidated by the gang to keep them in line. Kim said she became adept in the use of knives and even carried a gun. But she said she didn't like firearms.

"There was something about that gun that scared me," she said.

Her artistic skills were also put to use for the gang. Kim was a "tagger," one of the people who painted graffiti to mark gang territory and to show disrespect to other gangs by defacing their graffiti.

According to Kim, the gang provided her with security and a sense of family that her own family never did. But even that security wasn't enough to keep her in the gang when she realized she was going to have a family of her own.

When Kim became pregnant, she began to think about what kind of life she was going to provide her child. She knew that gang life would be inherently dangerous for her baby. That was made startlingly clear when she was about three months pregnant.

At that time, Kim was involved in a fight with a rival gang. During the fight, she was hit in the midsection many times. After it was over, she realized that she had potentially harmed a completely innocent person.

"I had put (the baby) through things that she couldn't even decide about," Kim said.

Fortunately, her unborn child was unhurt, but Kim had reached a crossroad in her life. She decided it was time for a change.

Today, Kim is a young woman determined to correct the mistakes of her past. She wants to provide her child the opportunities and sense of family she was denied by her own family. She wants to teach her baby that true fulfillment comes from having a stable home life and providing security for your children.

"If I can provide those skills for her, she won't have to adopt (a gang)," she said. "If I can do that I've succeeded."

Adult Attention Is Critical

Kim remains angry over her childhood. She said the best solution to the gang problem is for parents to take control. She points out that there were plenty of warning signs as she got deeper and deeper into the gang life.

Kim had gang symbols drawn on her backpacks, school books and clothing. Her style of dress, her language, almost every aspect of her life bespoke her gang affiliation. She said the fact that adults were afraid of confronting her, or wanted to be her friend, made entry into the gang that much easier.

"Don't be afraid to discipline your child. Children need to know where they stand," she said.

Kim credits boot camp programs and the Sea Cadets with turning her around. She said the strict authority and structured lifestyle gave her many things to think about and plenty of time to think. At the same time, graduating from the program provided a sense of accomplishment that can be built on.

"It gives the kid an identity," she said.

Having spent almost five years finding her identity in a gang, Kim hopes to prevent other teens from making the mistakes she made. While there were short-term benefits to being in the gang, she stressed that those benefits carried a very high price.

According to Kim, gang life is a painful existence that one can never truly leave behind. Most of her former gang comrades came from similar situations as hers. As she draws some gang symbols on a piece of paper, she explains what each line and jot means. The picture she draws is a heart, surrounded by a swirl of symbols and letters.

"That's our life," she says. "It shows the pain that surrounds our hearts."

The Emotional Problems of Gang Members

Lewis Yablonsky

Frequently coming from deprived families and blighted neighbor-hoods, young people who choose to join gangs are usually mar-ginal members of society at best, according to Lewis Yablonsky. In the following selection from his book *Gangsters: Fifty Years of Mad-ness, Drugs, and Death on the Streets of America*, Yablonsky exam-ines the typical emotional problems suffered by gang members, such as low self-esteem, insecurity, alienation, and hopelessness. In order to compensate for their poor self-image, the author explains, these youths may adopt a tough, macho persona. They often seek prestige and validation through senseless violence, he reports, acting out their rage against what they view as an unjust and hostile world. Yablonsky is a professor emeritus of sociology and criminology at California State University in Northridge.

A significant emotional factor that persists from the time of the early gangs and remains in the new violent-drug-gang equation is the sociopathic recklessness of gangster behavior, involving ruthless acts of violence with no concern for their victims and no remorse for their atrocious behavior. The hoods and barrios of America are heavily pop-ulated with teenagers and young adults whose poverty and depriva-tion have contributed to their ruthless emotional behavior.

Real and imagined territorial disputes remain a constant source of conflict between gangs. Gangbanging over territory is a weird cha-rade played out on the streets of America: gangsters, in fact, own nothing, especially their so-called territory. Many of these disputes are a pretext for acting out rage related to the gangsters' personal emotional problems.

Compensating Through "Machismo"

The gangsters' personality problems of low self-esteem and sense of alienation drive them to act super tough to compensate for their sense of inferiority. It produces what I term the "machismo" or "macho-syndrome." This syndrome is an effort to present themselves as a superman to compensate for their underlying feelings of low self-concept and of being "nobodies" in the larger society.

The macho-syndrome is characteristic of individuals who are so insecure about their masculinity that they behave at the opposite end of the continuum in a form of tough supermasculinity. This involves physically, emotionally, and verbally posturing as a machismolike superman. In the gangbangers' hoods or in any prison big yard, one can observe this extreme tough-guy behavior in action. Males with this syndrome don't simply walk, they move with an unmistakable superman strut. Emotionally and verbally, they are always engaged in proving their machismo. Any comment of disrespect to a gangster that implies femininity, like, "You're a pussy" or "You're a faggot," will quickly produce a violent response.

The gangster's macho-syndrome is an effort at compensating for his failure to succeed in the larger society. Youths with this affliction are usually failures in school and have no viable occupation. Gangsters have created their macho-syndrome stance in part as a reaction to their deeper feelings of alienation and hopelessness about achieving any degree of success in the larger society.

A Warped Sense of Community

Violent gangsters who feel alienated from the larger society create the gang to provide some sense of belonging to a "family," and a feeling of being somebody in their gang "community." The rage they feel from other sources is often expressed in gangbanging and other forms of senseless violence. The gang they have created outside of the law-abiding society offers them some kind of status in what they perceive as a barren and hopeless world.

On the subject of acquiring status through the gang, I had an interesting interview with a twenty-year-old gangster who was serving life in prison for a vicious murder. He told me how being known by his gang name Killer Ray was a great source of pride to him:

> Man, you don't know what I had to do to get this name. I love it. I put in the work for this name. People calling me Killer shows that they respect me, and they're not going to fuck with me. No one is going to "dis" Killer Ray, cause they know what will happen to them.

The phrase "putting in work" refers to the necessary violence, theft, and other delinquent behavior required to achieve status in the gang. In this context of acquiring a reputation and status in the gang, a gangbanger told me how he put in work at the scene of a gang murder that escalated his status in the gang:

> This dude was on the ground, and he wasn't dead yet. My homies and I were standing over him looking down at him. He was kind of moaning. I put the gun in his mouth and

smoked him. My homies never forgot what I did. Everyone talked about it for a long time. After that I was more accepted in the gang and I became known more as someone you don't ever fuck with.

An Alternative Source of Status

Seeking status in society through illegal means is imbedded in the sociological concept of "anomie." In my view, anomie is a most useful theory for explaining the social-psychological raison d'être [reason for being] for the existence of gangs in American society. Several sociologists, especially Emile Durkheim, Robert Merton, and, more recently, Richard Cloward and Lloyd Ohlin, have theorized about the concept of anomie. The theory posits that there is a disparity that exists between the idealized success goals and the means for achieving these goals in American society. When certain segments of the society accept and desire the society's goals, but because of limited opportunity cannot achieve these goals, they turn to deviant and illegal means for achieving the society's goals. I believe the contemporary gang is, in part, the alternative that has evolved from the status frustration of many minority youths who feel hopeless about achieving success through legitimate means in American society.

In this context, in the barrio or the hood their gang has become for many minority group youths their only achievable source of identity, status, and emotional satisfaction. Ill-trained to participate with any degree of success in the dominant middle-class world of rigid ideas, values, education, and adult demands, they construct their own pseudocommunity—the gang. In their gang, they can set achievable goals that can be realized through violent behavior. Their gang is an idealized empire, part real, part fantasy, that helps them endure the confusion of adolescence and the other emotional problems they confront in their separate and unequal world.

The violent gang becomes a haven for these emotionally needy youths, in part because it provides a vehicle through which they can act out their rage against what they perceive as an unfair and hostile world. They strike back through gang violence at a society they feel has boxed them into hopelessness. The gang for these youths is created as a deviant group for achieving the power, status, and respect that they believe, with some evidence, is denied them in the larger society.

The demands for performance and responsibility in the violent gang are readily adapted to the needs of these emotionally disabled youths. The criteria for membership is vague, yet easily possible when compared to the more demanding requirements of school or a job.

The Myth of the Gang as Family

Gangsters often claim that the gang is organized for protection and a feeling of having a family. This is often a hope and a myth rather than a reality. On too many occasions I have seen gangsters ready to snitch and give each other up to the police for some relief of their arrest situation. Their idealized behavioral family values are often quickly abandoned when it is to their personal advantage. Yet it is of emotional importance and solace to the gangster to believe that their gang is a family haven in the hostile world that surrounds them.

The Damien Williams case is one notable example that reflects the mythology of gang members' "hanging tough for their homies" and not snitching on them in order to perpetuate the myth of the gang as a family. Williams, an identified Crip gangster, was convicted of viciously assaulting an innocent truck driver, Reginald Denney, during the 1992 Los Angeles riots. During his trial I was called as an expert witness. The police who drove me to the courthouse told me that Williams, when he was apprehended, confessed to the crime in a taped interview. In the police station he began to cry, admitted his culpability in beating Denney, and expressed his strong motivation to implicate other gangsters who committed violent acts if the police would release him from custody or offer him a plea bargain. Williams's behavior is typical for most gangsters, who profess undying loyalty to their "familial" gang yet in actuality will quickly sell out their gangster "brothers" if it will serve their own, self-centered needs. (Williams's taped confession was not allowed into evidence in the trial because he had not been properly given the Miranda warning against self-incrimination by the police.)

A Lack of Humanity

The youth most susceptible to violent gang membership emerges from a social milieu that trains him inadequately for assuming a more constructive social role in the larger society. In fact, the defective socialization process to which he is subjected fosters a lack of humanistic feelings. At hardly any point is he trained to have feelings of compassion or responsibility for other people, not even for his partners in crime. Most gangsters, even when they are not certifiable sociopaths, at least in terms of their behavior outside of the gang, enact the sociopathic syndrome of senseless violence in their gangbanging behavior.

Gangbanging, the basic activity of one gang fighting another gang, is a standard cultural form for gangsters and reflects the limited compassion that is characteristic of the sociopathic gangster. A gangster can commit horrendous acts of violence in the context of gangbanging, and it is sanctioned by his gang. After a period of participating in a variety of dehumanized acts to achieve and solidify their rep in the gang, they tend to become unfeeling. They become insensitive to the pain of the violence they inflict on their victim. They develop a limited ability to identify or empathize with their victim or have any sense of remorse. Through this gang process of desensitizing their behavior, they become capable of committing spontaneous acts of senseless violence without feeling concern or guilt. I interviewed one gang member who had killed another boy, who gave a classic sociopathic comment that aptly describes this pattern of feeling, "What was I thinking about when I stabbed him? Man, are you crazy? I was thinking about whether to do it again!"

A common response that I have elicited from a number of gang-bangers in prison for murder involved the following dialogue:

LY: How do you now feel about the guy you murdered?

G: It's no big deal. He deserved it for dissing (disrespecting) me.

LY: Do you have any regrets?

G: Are you out of your fucking mind? Of course I have regrets. I'm here in the joint doing life!

Leadership in the violent gang is not acquired by a vote from his constituents. Leadership in the violent gang is achieved by continuing acts of the cool, unpredictable violence that is characteristic of gangbanging. One of the violent-gang leader's vital functions for other gang members is that he serves as a role model in the commission of an idealized form of violence. The leader is a shining example for gang followers. The leader has "heart" and will pull a trigger without any overt signs of fear or, most important, regret. As a prototype of the violent gang, the leader is thus an ideal role model. Free-floating violence, pure and unencumbered by social restrictions, rationality, conscience, or regret, characterizes the venerated, typical, heroic gang leader.

Prestige Through Violence

The selection of senseless violence by gangsters involves a curious logic. This form of violent behavior requires limited training, courage, personal ability, or even physical strength. As one gang boy commented, "Any kind of gun makes you ten feet tall." Because this pattern of senseless violence is a demonstration of easily achieved power, it is the paramount value of the violent gang.

The very fact that it is senseless rather than rational violence that appeals to gangsters reveals a great deal about the meaning of violence to them. It is an easy, quick, almost magical way of achieving power and prestige. In a single act of unpremeditated intensity, a gangster establishes a sense of his own identity and impresses this existence on others. No special ability is required to commit this brand of violence, not even a plan, and the guilt connected with the senseless violence is minimized by the gang's approval. This is especially true if the violence fulfills the gang's idealized standards of a swift, sudden, and senseless outbreak.

As indicated, gangsters lack the qualifications required for participation in more structured law-abiding organizations. Any youth in the gang's hood is easily accepted into the group. If qualifications for participation in the violent gang were more demanding, most gangsters, especially the more sociopathic leaders, would be unable to participate. The violent gang is thus a human collectivity where even the most emotionally and socially deficient and rejected youth is accepted and is able to acquire some success and status.

Seeking Validation

One aspect of the gangster's senseless violence is related to a concept I have termed "existential validation," or the validation of one's existence. This syndrome basically relates to the gangster's emotional alienation from human feeling or meaning. In contrast to the gangster, most people have a sense of identity and existence in their everyday activities. They do not require daily, intense, outrageous emotional excitement to know they are alive, that they exist. The sociopathic gangster, however, desires this kind of emotional excitement and intensity on a continuing basis. Their sense of boredom, and the feeling of an underlying insecurity about their masculinity, requires increasingly heavier dosages of bizarre and extreme violent behavior to validate the fact that they really exist and that they have some power in life.

Extreme, violent behavior is one activity that gives the sociopathic gangster a glimmer of feeling. Existential validation through violence (or other extremist bizarre behavior involving sex or drugs) gives many of these emotionally dead youths some feeling. As one gang killer told me, "When I stabbed him once, it felt good. I did it again and again because it made me feel alive."

Gang Pathology

Too often, erroneously, gang violence is attributed by the police and the media, from their more logical viewpoint, as being related to a more rational explanation of gang vengeance or retaliation. In fact, many acts defined as gang violence are really the individualistic behavior of a violent sociopath who may or may not have a strong gang affiliation. In this context, the term "gang-related" violence has come into vogue and is used almost daily in urban newspapers. Often this label has nothing to do with an actual gang homicide.

A media-identified gang-related murder may simply mean that a psychotic or sociopathic murderer, who has some peripheral gang affiliation, has committed a pathologically based, senseless act of homicide. Many victims of so-called gang-related murders (about 50 percent) are ordinary citizens of all ages who happen to innocently and tragically find themselves in the line of fire. The emotionally disordered sociopath who committed the murder may later claim a gang affiliation to mask his psychosis and give it a cloak of immunity.

Many murders characterized as gang related, therefore, may have very little connection to gang retaliation and more to do with a disturbed sociopath's paranoia. The murderer's self-identification as a gang member gives the emotionally disturbed killer a cloak of immunity from being considered just plain crazy. Being perceived as a gangster fighting for his homeboys and their territory is more likely to be considered a more rational and valorous act than being a crazy person carrying out a senseless act of murder.

Psychotics usually act out their pathology alone; the violent gang is comprised of a group of pathological individuals acting in concert. When a sociopathic gangster commits a senseless act of violence on his own, it is viewed as being pathological. However, the same act perpetrated with others, as, for example, in a drive-by murder, gives this maniacal activity a patina of rationality.

A brief appraisal of collective behavior patterns gives some clue to this element of group legitimization and sanction for bizarre and pathological group action. Sociologists Kurt and Gladys Lang make this point in a discussion of crowd behavior. They assert that certain aspects of a group situation help to make pathological acts and emotions acceptable. They write: "The principle that expressions of impulses and sentiments are validated by the social support they attract extends to collective expressions generally. The mere fact that an idea is held by a multitude of people tends to give it credence." In the violent gang, when all the gangsters "go crazy together," as in gang warfare, their behavior tends, at least in the viewpoint of some people, to have greater rationality. Gang "legitimacy" therefore partially derives from the fact that group behavior, however irrational, is generally not considered as pathological as the solo act of an individual.

Suicidal Tendencies

In this context of emotionally disordered behavior, many gangsters who commit gang-related murders, in my view, are pathological and have suicidal personalities. Most gangsters have low self-esteem, and this is reflected in their suicidal tendencies. They continually place themselves in the line of deadly gunfire that may come from an enemy gang or a police bullet.

Father Gregory Boyle, the director of a gang-prevention program in the East L.A. parish of his Dolores Mission Church, sees gangbanging in the same way I do, as a form of pathological and suicidal behavior. In an article, "Hope Is the Only Antidote," he comments,

> The week before Christmas, I had to bury the 40th young person killed by what is still a plague in my Eastside community. I've grown weary of saying that gangbanging is the urban poor's version of teen-age suicide. The violence that has us in its grip has always indicated larger problems: poverty, unemployment, racism, the great disparity between the haves and

have-nots, dysfunctional families and above all, despair. And for our neglect in addressing these problems as we ought, it shouldn't surprise us that their symptomatic manifestations have only worsened. This week, I will bury a homeboy who, unable to find his way clear to imagine a future—put a gun to his temple and ended his life. This desperate act of an 18-year-old sidestepped the inner city's more acceptable mode of suicide—the irrational battlefield of a gang war. He chose instead to make explicit the wish for death long implicit among our youth.

Committing suicide explicitly reveals the manifestation of an inner emotional pathology. As indicated, being a gangster is a more highly desirable pathological syndrome than many other patterns that are viewed with greater opprobrium in society. The person who is in a position to accept the gang front for his pathology is not generally considered as crazy as someone who babbles a verbal word salad. Even more advantageous is the fact that as a gangbanger he has found an acceptable macho public role in his own community that is to some extent validated in the violent larger society.

WHY GIRLS JOIN GANGS

Paul Palango

Girls with low self-esteem—particularly those who have been raised in dysfunctional families or who have been physically or sexually abused—are often vulnerable to the lure of gangs, Paul Palango reports in the following selection. These troubled girls have an intense need for acceptance and love, he notes, yet they typically feel unwanted by their families and rejected by their schoolmates. Unable to find the emotional support they need, these young women take refuge in the gang lifestyle, which provides them with an outlet to express their rebellion, frustration, and rage. Palango is an investigative journalist and the author of *Above the Law* and *The Last Guardians*.

What first scares many parents is the music. Their daughter has just become a teenager and almost overnight, it seems, her taste has changed from Raffi to gangsta rap, the street music of the black ghettos in the United States. The little girl who once rollicked to Baby Beluga and Down by the Bay has, at the age of 12 or 13, become desperate to attract boys and win acceptance from other girls. She's taking endless showers to lyrics such as these from the popular *High School High* movie sound track: "Blow your head off"; "Let's get it on like Smith and Wesson"; "Kill a nigger for my nigger"—and far worse.

This is the music du jour of many young North American teenagers these days—the evocation of sexual abuse, violence and death. But the music usually is only a manifestation of something more sinister, lurking deep inside many young girls. For the damaged and insecure, the songs serve as a diabolical road map to the girls' own private hell.

Many come from dysfunctional families. Many are the daughters of alcohol and drug abusers, or have been physically or sexually abused, or, according to recent medical research, have suffered undetected brain injuries from childhood accidents.

Unable to function properly in society, these girls have low self-esteem, as did Reena Virk, the Saanich, British Columbia murder victim [who was beaten and drowned by seven teenage girls and one teenage boy on November 14, 1997]. Virk had the added burden of not being conventionally pretty. As a result, she was the object of taunting and bullying at her new school. It is not a new phenomenon. It happens every year, in the meanest housing projects and the fanciest private schools. There is even a fascinating 1996 film about the subject, *Welcome to the Dollhouse*. The central character is a homely girl named Dawn Wiener who is so desperate for affection that she shows up repeatedly to meet a bad boy who keeps threatening to rape her—but, in the end, even he rejects her.

There was a little of Dawn Wiener in Reena Virk, who wanted to be accepted by her chosen peers, a wanna-be Los Angeles–style street gang. They were into gangsta rap, shoplifting and violence. But they did not want Reena. They tried to stub a cigarette out on her forehead, they beat her brutally and left her to drown.

One Girl's Descent

Meet Kathleen. A few years ago, she could have met the same end as Reena. Unlike Reena, Kathleen (not her real name) came from a middle-class family in the Ottawa area. Tall and gangly, and with a poor self-image, she had studied ballet as a child, but never excelled at anything. She had been sexually abused as a small child, although her family was unaware of it until after she hit bottom in a descent that began in Grade 9. She was 14, and found she couldn't successfully compete for the attention of boys. Older, bigger and tougher girls began to taunt and bully her. Kathleen stopped going to school and began hanging out in coffee shops and at the downtown Rideau Centre mall, just below Parliament Hill.

She took refuge in gangsta rap. Her favorites were Niggers With Attitude, Public Enemy and Ice T., whose narcotic-like chants and rhythms masked the malevolence of their lyrics. Their songs were paeans to violence, to killing police and degrading women.

The clues to Kathleen's descent were subtle at first, lost in the confusion of hormonal change and the widely held myth that most teenagers instantly become rebellious once they turn 13. The first tip-off might have been when Kathleen shed her old and dear childhood friends. Although this change might not seem abnormal for someone moving from elementary to high school, experts say it is often the first visible marker in the destabilization of a personality. "I started to see them as Goody Two-shoes and nerds," Kathleen says. "On Friday nights, they stayed home and watched videos. I started hanging around with a girl who drank, but that was about it. She wasn't really a bad person." The friendship did not last long, however. Soon, Kathleen took up with Fay, a tougher, streetwise girl who not only drank but also did drugs. This tiered descent from childhood friends to unstable street acquaintances is typical of psychologically distressed teenagers, according to Richmond Hill, Ont., behavioral specialist Ruth Whitham.

Unlike Kathleen, Fay came from a broken home. Her mother had been married four times and had run an escort service out of their house. Fay became Kathleen's mentor and guide to the underworld. As she looks back at herself now, Kathleen remembers having no emotions—an almost sociopathic view of the world. "I had no respect for or fear of authority," she recalls. And, she says, she was completely "disinhibited"—a clinical term to describe a person who is incapable of feeling embarrassment or shame. "I would do and say anything. I didn't give a damn."

Kathleen adopted the culture depicted in the rap songs as her own. That culture grew out of grinding poverty, the lack of a political voice and the oppression of white police. Yet the rebellion and rage of the ghettos hold a curious appeal for some vulnerable nonblack teens. "We really got into this black thing," Kathleen says. "It's funny. I'm fair-skinned, but I desperately wanted to be black. I started dressing like a home-girl and talking the talk. When I was 14, I even told my mother that my goal was to have a baby with a black guy by the time I was 15."

As the pattern of collapse continued, the shoplifting began. "It wasn't because I couldn't afford the clothes, because I could," she says. "I stole clothes to wear to the clubs—short skirts and bra tops that my mother wouldn't let me wear." Kathleen and Fay also hooked up with a group of criminally minded men, most of them black. She would go back to their apartments, do drugs, have sex and allow herself to be flattered. Desperately in need of love and acceptance, she was an all-too-willing victim.

The Ottawa street scene in the early to mid-1990s was typical of what was happening in other Canadian and U.S. cities. Out of nowhere violent gangs, many of them female, arose, with names such as the Scorpions, Nasty Girls and Bitches With Attitude. Kathleen became intimate with the gang world. "All you do is think about yourself, but you have no real feelings or emotions," she says. "No conscience and no judgment. I desperately wanted to be popular and the way to be popular was to do anything the gang leader wanted. If a guy told me I was pretty, I would go to bed with him. If my gang leader told me to beat someone up, I beat them up. I was always trying to feel tough and superior. After a while, you start to believe that you actually are the people in the songs."

Kathleen's Parents Intervene

Kathleen hit bottom when she was 15. Her gang leader had ordered her to become a prostitute on the streets of Ottawa. "I only did it two times before my parents realized what was going on and took control." After a brief stay in an Ottawa detention centre, she was sent to a rehabilitation centre in Minnesota that specializes in psychiatry and addiction. (There is no comparable institution in Canada.) "My mom told me it was going to be like a Holiday Inn, but it was like a jail,"

Kathleen says. "They brainwashed me—but it was for the good. They made me feel guilty. I got my judgment and conscience back."

For Kathleen and her family, perhaps the most important development from the Minnesota experience was that she confronted her repeated sexual abuse by a neighborhood boy when she was about five years old. Her parents never knew. "I never told them because I was embarrassed about it," she says. Her family saved her: "My parents each almost had a nervous breakdown and almost got divorced over me. It cost them $30,000 to get me treated, but I am one of the lucky ones. I have a family who cared for me. If they hadn't intervened, I probably would be dead now."

But she survived—and, having put those days behind her, changed her life around almost as completely as her hairstyle and clothes. That is not untypical, says Kathleen's lawyer, Carey MacLellan, who over the years has represented many of Ottawa's youth in criminal matters. "For girls, there is an intensity to their involvement, a completeness that is different from boys. More often than not, a boy will be involved in crime but will also be hanging around school and doing a little schoolwork with some degree of normalcy. When it comes to changing their behavior, boys talk about changing, but it's usually only a lot of lip service," MacLellan notes. "The girls tend to go right at it. When they make up their mind to change, they change completely."

In Burnaby, British Columbia, Royal Canadian Mounted Police Inspector Dennis Schlecker agrees. Over the years, he has investigated a number of murders. "It has been my experience that in most cases violent girls don't stay violent," Schlecker says. "When an 11-year-old boy kills someone in a horrible way, there's usually no hope for him. He's a lost cause. With girls it's different. They have an entirely different thought process."

Today, Kathleen is in university, doing exceptionally well, and hopes one day to become a police officer. "I look back at those days and the influence the rap music had on me, and I can't believe how I could have been influenced," she says. "It was all about the degradation of women, but I couldn't see that at the time."

Kathleen's middle-class parents had the money and connections to save her. But, says MacLellan, "for every one who does change, there are a hundred who aren't functioning very well in society." Reena Virk was one of those—right to her gruesome and terrible end.

CHAPTER 5

MEASURES TO REDUCE AND PREVENT GANG ACTIVITY

GOVERNMENT EFFORTS IN GANG PREVENTION

Office of Juvenile Justice and Delinquency Prevention

Because gangs have traditionally been concentrated in distinct neighborhoods and communities, gang prevention efforts have largely been local in focus. Recently, however, there has been an escalation of state and federal anti-gang efforts, as well as growing cooperation between different government jurisdictions in the fight against gangs. The following selection, taken from a 1997 report by the U.S. Department of Justice's Office of Juvenile Justice and Delinquency Prevention, highlights and assesses the effectiveness of various federal, state, and local governmental initiatives aimed at reducing the spread of gangs.

Gang problems traditionally have been local, urban problems, and governmental responses to gang problems traditionally have been focused at the local level. Yet, while the past decade has been marked by the spread of gangs and gang-related violence, it has also seen the growing confluence of Federal, State, and local efforts to control gang activity and reduce gang violence. Moreover, it has seen the rise of more proactive, community-based strategies for dealing with gangs.

Three general strategies for preventing gangs have been evaluated: preventing youth from joining gangs, transforming existing gangs into neighborhood clubs, and mediating and intervening in conflicts between gangs. Of the three approaches, prevention programs that integrate school curriculums with afterschool recreational activities seem to hold the most promise for preventing gang crime and violence.

In areas where gang problems are endemic, such as Los Angeles County, prevention and intervention strategies combined with long-term, proactive investigations of entire gangs work better than reactive, short-term investigations and prosecutions of individual gang members.

State Initiatives

States have done their part in the fight against gangs by enhancing penalties for gang-related crime and fostering cooperation between jurisdictions and disciplines. Illinois, for example, has adopted a coordinated, holistic approach to addressing gang problems. In 1995, Governor Jim Edgar established by executive order the 35-member Governor's Commission on Gangs, with Attorney General Jim Ryan serving as chairman. The commission was composed of Federal and State prosecutors, police, educators, parents, clergy, health professionals, lawmakers, and representatives of business and labor.

The commission has held 16 public hearings, a youth forum, and a 2-day conference at locales across the State, gathering testimony from nearly 150 witnesses. As a result of commission findings and recommendations, the Governor, in June 1996, signed legislation drafted by the commission establishing a witness protection program. He also appropriated $1 million for a pilot program to protect victims and witnesses who testify against gang members. The new law includes strict sanctions for gang members who commit crimes, including an imposition of harsher penalties for gang leaders convicted of drug dealing and mandatory reporting of any firearm-related incidents at public schools to law enforcement within 24 hours. The commission is expected to issue a report that will stress the need for get-tough measures balanced by more intervention and prevention programs.

Another recent antigang measure from Illinois creates offenses for compelling another to join a gang or deterring resignation from a gang. Moreover, the State has enacted a law that prohibits a person who has coerced another to join a gang from receiving probation, a conditional discharge, or periodic imprisonment.

Enhanced sentencing is yet another State response to combating crime committed by gangs and gang members. Arkansas and California, among other States, have increased the penalties for specific gang-related violence, such as drive-by shootings. In September 1996, California Governor Pete Wilson signed a law extending indefinitely the California Street Terrorism Enforcement and Prevention Act, which enhances penalties for gang-related activities.

Other States have enacted statutes that enhance penalties for any criminal act committed by a gang member. For example, Tennessee enacted a law that adds criminal street gang membership as an enhancement factor for sentencing defendants who have committed a prior offense within the past 3 years. Provisions of a Nevada law include forfeiture of personal property that has been used in a gang crime and authorize schools to enforce antigang rules and develop gang-prevention programs.

Local jurisdictions have a number of law enforcement approaches to controlling gang activity and reducing gang-related crime. Cities have passed ordinances prohibiting cruising, loitering, and many forms of belligerent public behavior, such as discharging weapons on private property, consuming alcohol in public, and playing loud music. Other cities have cracked down on graffiti and other forms of vandalism by regulating the sale, purchase, or possession of materials used to deface property and by adopting parental responsibility laws that make parents liable for the damage illegally caused by their children. Still other cities closely enforce truancy and curfew ordinances.

Some cities have attempted to discourage gang membership by prohibiting behavior that manifests gang membership, such as wearing gang colors or using gestures that communicate gang affiliation. For example, the city of Harvard, IL, prohibits individuals from wearing gang-related colors, emblems, or insignia in public or from making any utterances or gestures that communicate gang membership or insult to other street gangs. Since the ordinance became effective, the number of gang-related arrests has decreased from 87 in 1994 to 0 as of July 11, 1996.

To control gang-related violence in and near public housing projects, housing authorities are authorized by the U.S. Department of Housing and Urban Development (HUD) to insert provisions into leases prohibiting the use, display, or possession of firearms. Gang members or family members and associates of gang members face eviction if caught using or possessing guns. Cities also have passed temporary ordinances banning access by gang members to public parks that have been the sites of confrontations between gangs.

Other cities have sought civil injunctions against gangs as "unincorporated associations" that prohibit targeted gang members from congregating in certain areas. Prosecutors in Los Angeles and nearby cities have implemented four gang injunctions, serving gang members with court documents and discussing with them activities prohibited by the court. Before a civil injunction against the Blythe Street Gang in April 1993, drive-by shootings were a weekly occurrence and a neighborhood grocery store was forced to close down. Since the injunction, the store is back, and at least a year has passed between drive-by shootings. A local community organization has received a major grant to make improvements to the neighborhood.

Multijurisdictional Initiatives

Many counties and cities have found success in pooling resources with Federal and State agencies to fight and control gangs and gang-related violence. With the size and diversity of its gang problem, California, particularly Los Angeles County, has become a national leader in developing and implementing gang initiatives that draw on both Federal and local resources.

An estimated 150,000 members belong to more than 1,000 gang factions in the Los Angeles area, according to media reports. The *Los Angeles Times* reported that gang-related murders have accounted for roughly 40 percent of homicides in Los Angeles County in recent years. Although there has been an on-again, off-again truce between the two major gang divisions, the Crips and the Bloods, since the rioting surrounding the Rodney King verdict in the summer of 1992, gang-related violent crime continues to plague the region.

As a response, Federal officials, in cooperation with local law enforcement authorities, launched the largest crackdown ever on Los Angeles gangs. They called their effort the Los Angeles Metropolitan Task Force (LA Task Force). The LA Task Force increased law enforcement efforts to combat violent gang crime—the FBI increased the number of agents who investigate gangs and gang-related crimes from about 74 to 100; the U.S. attorney's office brought in an experienced gang prosecutor; and the local Bureau of Alcohol, Tobacco and Firearms (ATF) office announced plans to hire another 10 agents, largely to investigate gang members.

By using Federal racketeering laws and other tactics such as wiretapping, Federal and local officials attempted to break down gang factions, including State prison gangs, which contribute to the drug dealing and violence that plague the inner-city areas. Federal sentencing laws are more stringent than State laws, and because there is no Federal parole, convicted felons serve their full sentences. Gang members can also be spread across the Federal system rather than being housed in State prisons where many of their fellow inmates may have been members of their gang outside prison walls.

As part of a self-initiated review of the effort, the U.S. General Accounting Office (GAO) interviewed 37 members of local law enforcement agencies who had participated in the LA Task Force. The participants were asked which investigative methods worked best, if Federal contributions had been useful, and if multijurisdictional cooperation had been helpful in reducing gang violence.

Participants reported that Federal assistance to Los Angeles law enforcement had been helpful in fighting the area's gang epidemic and was used for wiretapping and witness protection under Federal rules, overtime pay, equipment, office space, and money for informants and undercover purchases of drugs and firearms.

Most of the 24 line officers interviewed pointed to the task force's focus on long-term investigations of entire gangs, rather than reactive investigations of individual gang members, as a key to the LA Task Force's success. According to statistics provided to GAO, the LA Task Force was responsible for more than 2,000 arrests—almost half for violent crimes—between February 1992 and September 1995. Three-fourths of all Federal and State convictions coming from task force arrests were for violent crimes. GAO did not independently verify the statistics.

The LA Task Force was cited as an example of an effective program targeting violent crime in the U.S. Department of Justice's *Attorney*

General's Progress Report to the President on the Anti-Violent Crime Initiative, released in September 1996. In particular, the Attorney General's report mentioned a 1-day effort in 1995 that resulted in a 57-percent drop in violent crime in one Los Angeles neighborhood.

The effort, called Operation Sunrise, was the result of more than 2 years of joint investigation of activities by the Eight Trey Gangster Crips. The gang made up less than 1 percent of the community's population but accounted for more than 80 percent of the area's violent crime, according to the GAO report. During the operation, Federal and local agents swept a 30-by-30-block area of South Central Los Angeles controlled by the gang, serving 120 search warrants in 1 day. The operation resulted in several Federal and State prosecutions, the confiscation of 67 firearms and 2,000 rounds of ammunition, and the seizure of 2 kilograms of methamphetamine.

Other Combined Efforts

Other initiatives that bring together Federal, State, and local resources and manpower are being tried across the country. Some of these efforts were highlighted in the Attorney General's progress report, including the following:

• In Michigan, the Safe Streets–Violent Crime Task Force conducted an investigation of the Home Invaders, a gang that had gained entrance to more than 100 homes in the Detroit area while posing as police officers. Twenty-two members were indicted on charges under the Federal Racketeer Influenced and Corrupt Organizations (RICO) and Violent Crimes in Aid of Racketeering statutes and for weapons possession.

• In Rhode Island, a Federal and State task force conducted a 21-month investigation of the Latin Kings called Operation Check. The task force, which was sponsored by the ATF, included State and local police, State corrections officers, the Rhode Island National Guard, the FBI, HUD, the U.S. Department of the Treasury, the U.S. Secret Service, and the Immigration and Naturalization Service (INS). The probe led to an 18-count RICO indictment against 11 Latin Kings. Four defendants had pleaded guilty as of September 1996. The rest were awaiting trial.

• In New York, a task force composed of the FBI, the U.S. Drug Enforcement Agency, INS, the U.S. attorney's office in Buffalo, the New York State Police, the Erie County Sheriff's Department, the Erie County and Genesee County district attorney's offices, and the police departments of Rochester, Amherst, and Buffalo conducted an 18-month investigation of several drug trafficking organizations and street gangs. Using court-authorized wiretaps, undercover operations, and other investigative techniques, the joint task force probe resulted in the indictment of 71 defendants, including the leader of the Goodyear Crew, a street gang operating in Buffalo. Forty defendants have pleaded guilty, and the rest were awaiting trial, as of September 1996.

Gang Prosecution

While specialized gang units are common in police departments of cities with gang problems, they are less common in prosecutors' offices. Those that have been established have begun to use a "vertical prosecution" process, whereby one attorney, or a group of attorneys, stays with a case from inception to conclusion. In California, several jurisdictions have combined vertical prosecution strategies with a type of proactive community policing-like prosecution.

Whereas reactive prosecution means responding to crimes and closed investigations, a prosecutor's office using a proactive, community prosecution strategy attempts to stop the crime before it occurs or at least attempts to participate in the initial investigation. Instances of the former can include using city ordinances to force absentee landlords to clean up, fix up, or close down suspected crack houses. Examples of the latter include going with police to interview victims and witnesses, talking to gang members, and taking steps to protect witnesses. The San Diego County, CA, district attorney's office has a gang unit that has served as a national model for this approach.

JOB-SKILLS TRAINING FOR GANG MEMBERS

Carol Ann Morrow

In the following article, Carol Ann Morrow profiles Jesuit priest Greg Boyle, who has been involved in ministry outreach to the gang members of East Los Angeles since 1986. Known as Father Greg by his constituents, Boyle's primary focus is on job-skills development, Morrow explains, which he promotes as a method of empowering gang members to better their lives. As part of his Jobs for a Future program, Boyle operates Homeboy Industries, which produces clothing and novelty items, and Homeboy Bakery, which supplies fine restaurants with baked goods. Gang members who work in the Homeboy businesses develop skills that assist them in obtaining legitimate employment and breaking free of the gang lifestyle, the author writes. Morrow is the assistant managing editor for *St. Anthony Messenger*, a monthly Catholic magazine.

It helps to have connections if you want to meet the Rev. Greg Boyle, S.J.—gang connections. Father Greg doesn't have much time to tell his story to *St. Anthony Messenger*. Why? Because he gives—and gives and gives—his time, his energy and his influence (known in the neighborhood as "juice") to the young people of the Pico/Aliso District in East L.A.

Pico Gardens and Aliso Village, sometimes called "The Projects," is the largest tract of subsidized housing west of the Mississippi. This huge piece of social engineering hasn't worked out so well. It's poor, crowded and packed with gangs.

Some of Pico/Aliso overlaps Boyle Heights (different era, different Boyle). Within those 16 square miles, 60 gangs claim 10,000 members, Hispanic and black. This equals violence and plenty of action at the Hollenbeck division of the Los Angeles Police Department—if Father Greg Boyle doesn't get there first.

Saving Youths at Light Speed

In two days hanging around Father Greg's office, a modest though vividly painted storefront on L.A.'s East First Street, G-Dog or G, as the kids affectionately call the Jesuit priest, reveals life in a very fast lane. The priest's office—nine feet square maximum—is a windowless, unfinished drywall box in the epicenter of the 600-square-foot headquarters of Jobs for a Future (JFF). He has an open door in—and an open door beyond—to other offices, storage for Homeboy Industries silkscreened items and the only bathroom. Traffic through Greg's doorway feels as hectic as the L.A. freeway system.

Father Greg requests, "Hold my calls." But when a prison inmate gets a chance to phone, the priest reneges, "Well, let me take just this one. . . ." A young man comes by—dressed for success—to tell his happy story and thank Father Greg for the contact, the clothes, a job, a hope. With Greg on the phone and me in the visitor's chair, the young man preens back and forth between the front and back doors of this short runway. He and the priest exchange a complex handshake, a triumphant smile, a thumbs-up. No words seem necessary. Pride is evident in both son—and father. Father Greg is surrogate parent to hundreds of Hispanic youth, many the children of Latino immigrants.

The office is crammed with memorabilia which I study while he's on the phone. Official framed certificates, plaques and news clippings hang next to drawings by—and photos of—neighborhood youth. Latin American artifacts and activist posters jockey for wall space with strong, distinctive samples of graffiti wall art. The colorful sketches Father Greg has pinned to the wall have no ominous overtones, however. His poorly lit office is bright with evidence of love.

How can Father Greg take time to talk about what's already happened when more is happening—right now? How can he speak of his dreams when young dreamers are lined up outside the door? "So—what do you want to know?" he asks as he hangs up the phone, signs some kind of permission slip for a girl's school function, hollers out with pseudo-sternness, "No more calls!" and tries to fit the story of his life into the 10 minutes before he dashes to another appointment.

An Irish-American Jesuit Homeboy

Gregory Boyle is one of eight children. His father, third-generation Irish-American, worked in a family-founded dairy in Los Angeles County. His mom worked to keep track of her large family. When the young Greg graduated from L.A.'s Loyola High School in 1972, he decided to become a Jesuit and was ordained a priest in 1984.

To this observer, it would seem that the Jesuit's every assignment (pre- and post-ordination) would present major hurdles for most middle-class Americans: hospice, soup kitchen, prison, Latin America, the South Bronx. For Father Greg, each contributed to the pastoral awareness he brought to his 1986 assignment as pastor of Dolores Mission. He wanted to be a Jesuit because the Order has a social-activist bent. He wanted, he had said, to work with the poor. Dolores Mission is certainly that. The parish is within walking distance of downtown Los Angeles, yet constitutes another economic and social hemisphere.

It's been a bumpy 13 years for Father Greg, including a year and a half away from the neighborhood after his six years as pastor were concluded. Some people didn't want him to come back after his sabbatical, but they weren't the young men—and young women—who constituted the priest's primary focus: gang members and other kids on the edge.

Juggling Responsibilities

When he returned in 1994, his assignment was to concentrate exclusively on job development and related ministries with neighborhood gangs—and not on the other urgencies Los Angeles's poorest pastorate had required of him. JFF is more than enough to stress a much larger staff than the seven the agency employs.

Is he tired? It seems a logical question, given the pace observed in just two days! The 45-year-old Jesuit answers, "I don't expect to be doing this forever, but I love it and it gives me life. Like this morning—I'm coming from court and a kid flags me down and he's wearing his shirt unbuttoned, a nice dress shirt, nice pants. He's got a tie and he's waving it. 'Do my tie,' he's begging. So I pull over because it's an *emergency*. I do his tie and he looks great and I say, 'You know what, Johnny. I'm proud of you!' Johnny turns around and says, 'Me, too!'"

When he isn't fixing ties or talking on the phone, Father Greg may be in court—as he was this morning—or visiting the 14 detention centers where he celebrates Mass on a rotating basis, or out raising funds through a combination of great stories, hard truths and gospel witness. He might be out on the street. He might be writing letters, since he answers every letter from a local youth in detention. This averages about 40 a month, reports Celeste Fremon, in her thick and thrilling 1995 biography, *Father Greg & the Homeboys*. Her book is based on two years of following G-Dog around in good times and bad.

Both Doubted and Revered

Ms. Fremon, journalist, mother, advocate for Greg and the kids known as *homeboys* (Hispanic slang for the kids on one's own block or in one's gang; also known as *homies*), has heard the Los Angeles Police Department complain vociferously about Father Greg. They think he harbors and supports criminals. She has attended some of the many gang-member funerals over which Father Greg's presided. She's heard—and reported—the objections of police officers who say he glorifies gang membership by allowing Church burials for these young people. Greg sees a funeral as a great personal heartache but also a significant teaching moment, a time when other homies might let down their defenses and listen.

Celeste Fremon sees Father Greg as one of the neighborhood's greatest hopes. She describes Pico/Aliso as a war zone. She sees gang leaders as the kids with the "most intelligence, social skills, leadership capacity and the ability not to blink in the face of danger." She says that the Jesuit hasn't brought peace to Pico/Aliso but he has brought change. He has brought such an infusion of love that some young men "have finally become strong enough to save themselves," the concluding sentence of Ms. Fremon's book.

Father Greg is often interviewed on gang issues for radio and TV. He's been featured on *60 Minutes* and in *People Weekly*. Fremon's book, published by Hyperion Press, captured a piece of the priest's story between hard covers. Now comes a movie—or at least a script. A fellow Jesuit priest, Bill Cain of *Nothing Sacred* fame, has completed a screenplay for Columbia Pictures. Since Father Bill once lived at Dolores Mission, he didn't have to reach far for the exciting elements of plot and characterization. A production schedule—and the challenge of casting—still awaits.

A Talented and Energetic Staff

Father Greg has brought other dynamic and dedicated people to work at Jobs for a Future. Emily Castillo, Norma Gillette, John Tostado and Carlos Vasquez are also hard at work at JFF's First Street offices.

These staff members do what it takes to get kids working. Just what is that? Emily arranges for a "Clean Slate," which at JFF means getting tattoos removed. White Memorial Hospital doctors cooperate in this venture. Norma develops resumés and matches those resumés with job opportunities. She is scouring the want ads when I arrive, circling possibilities.

John and Carlos are job developers and case managers for youth in their early days of employment. They write letters of recommendation. They visit businesses to see how they can connect the energy of their clients with the goals of businesspeople.

JFF helps its clients get the clothes they need to make that all-important first impression. Father Greg spent part of this interview on the phone checking his credit balance, apparently finding the totals disappointing. "A million and one kids need clothes to get to jobs and stuff like that," he says, happily exasperated by a positive problem. Gilbert, a neighborhood youth now employed, is new at his job and "still pretty pushed for clothes." White T's and black Dickey work pants, de rigueur in the neighborhood, are—for that very reason—seldom admired in the workplace. Father Greg and other staff members also serve as tie-knot tutors and are happy to add that to their resumés.

To ensure employment opportunities, Father Greg began Homeboy Industries, which markets T-shirts, sweats, mugs and hats bearing the Homeboy logo. All these items are imprinted by Homeboy Silkscreen, a for-profit subsidiary.

A visit to the silkscreen operation and to Homeboy Bakery—both hot as blazes on an L.A. August afternoon—finds members of rival gangs sweating side by side, learning skills they can use and building a resumé that can also boast of their punctuality, reliability and ability to cooperate. While the bakery employs only 10 on a shift, young men can begin there, learn and move on. The men I see have no time to talk. They are intent on creating loaves of fragrant, yeasty, gourmet bread.

Carlos Vasquez explains that these are transitional, training businesses, but both appear to be succeeding. The bakery, oddly enough, failed as a tortilla supplier, but is getting good press in its current reincarnation as a supplier to fine restaurants with Frisco Baking Co. as distributor. KPWR, an L.A. hip-hop FM station, has given the bakery $150,000 through its Knowledge Is Power Foundation. It also engages the silkscreeners to make logo T's.

Three more companies are in place: Homeboy Landscaping, Homeboy Cleaning Service and Homeboy Artesania, which offers a cross and Christmas decorations. . . .

Why These Gangs?

The Los Angeles Police Department's anti-gang program is called Operation Hammer. The general approach is to get gang members off the street and into jail. Father Greg calls it the "full-incarceration method" which he contrasts with his own "full-employment strategy."

What explains this powerful and dangerous phenomenon of youth gangs? Father Greg says, "It's a sense of belonging. There's not something that *pulls* kids into gangs so much as something that *pushes* them. It's not so much what lures or attracts them but what pushes them out of the four walls that should be holding them in—and don't."

He continues, "The kid is sort of pushed out at home and then gravitates around this group. He's not so much, 'Wow, doesn't that look attractive.' It's *not*, because they will join a gang and they'll have to watch their back forever. They'll endanger the lives of their loved ones and it goes on and on. None of it is very attractive. But if there's abuse or alcohol or neglect or if the parents aren't around," kids look for a place they can belong.

They are high-spirited young people, wary but clever and charming. Armando Avecedo has a tattoo on his neck in Chinese characters. Why? He explains, "So not everyone can read it." How does it translate? "Trust no woman," he says deadpan, his dark eyes delighting in the irony of telling so many his secret.

"We are prone as a society to demonize and reject these kids and not want to help them," laments Father Greg. "What if we really were to deal with the problem rather than just resign ourselves to warehousing the consequences? What if we were just to say yes to kids rather than insist that kids just say no to gangs? We want adults to be able to say yes to these kids, to offer them a way to get on with their lives. They've been through a lot. I've never met a victimizer who wasn't first victimized. So you have to deal with that compassionately as Jesus would."

Imagining a Future

Jobs for a Future—and the mission of Greg Boyle—is premised on just that: a belief in the future, a future for each and every young person in the projects. Father Greg works with kids whose homes are broken, whose parents are unemployed, who have dropped out of school, who say they "ain't got no future." To them, the Jesuit says, "I can see your future! Trust me!" He explains that much of his ministry is to imagine a future that the kids can't see—and help that future materialize.

I ask for a success story: kids employed, kids grown and out of the projects, kids living the American dream. He points to young men working around the office, answering the constantly ringing phones, packaging Homeboy Industries orders, showing up for work, being "go-fers," being counted. "All the different gangs are represented right now in our office," he observes. "Not only does society need to put a human face on gangs but enemies also need to put a human face on one another," he adds.

Still Father Greg is hesitant to speak in terms of success. "I feel called to be faithful, not successful," he says. "I feel called to be faithful to an approach and to a certain wisdom about who these kids are. I believe that if they are given a chance, then they'll thrive and they'll begin to imagine a future for themselves."

What would this future look like? "Obviously, we want peace in the community. We want the kids to have a sense of who they are in God's eyes. They're such damaged kids in the sense that they haven't had much love or support at home. That affects their sense of themselves, of who they think they are.

"They think they're the bad son. I keep telling them over and over, 'You are the son that any parents would be proud to claim as their own.' That's the truth. That's not some fantasy. As soon as they know that they're exactly what God had in mind when God made them, then they become that. Then they like who they are. Once they can do that—love themselves—they're not inclined to shoot somebody or hurt somebody or be out there gang-banging."

They are the prized—if prodigal—sons. Jesuit Greg Boyle extends to them—and to many a homegirl as well—the accepting arms of a loving father.

STREET INTERVENTION

Alona Wartofsky

In the following article, *Washington Post* staff writer Alona Wartofsky examines the work of Barios Unidos (United Neighborhoods), an organization whose mission is to prevent gang members from committing crimes and violence. In particular, Wartofsky looks at the Washington, D.C., chapter of Barios Unidos and its controversial founder Luis Cardona, himself a former gang member. Cardona takes his message directly to the streets, she explains, often patrolling gang-infested neighborhoods to recruit youths for the chapter's meetings, to provide safe rides home to teenagers who are out late, or to break up fights between gang members. Some local authorities are critical of the type of street intervention that Cardona employs, the author notes, while others believe that at-risk teens respond well to such efforts.

Just before midnight, a white Nissan Pathfinder packed with teenagers cruises the Mount Pleasant neighborhood of Washington, D.C. The driver slows as he approaches a crew of young men huddled on a street corner. He rolls down his window. "Hey! Go home!"

The street hustlers nod noncommittally. Then one of them breaks ranks:

"Luis! Can we ride with you?"

The Pathfinder is already filled beyond capacity, its windows fogged by the warmth of so many bodies.

"Nah man, I'm full. Go home!"

The Pathfinder peels off, but a few minutes later, Luis Cardona drives past the group again. One of the hustlers sees him coming and ducks out of view. "Look," says Cardona. "This [expletive] is trying to hide behind that trash can. Like we can't see him." He shakes his head and smiles. The kids in the car giggle.

Jose Marquez, 19, left his parents' house when he was 14 and has been kicked out of so many high schools he can't remember them all. Jimila Simmons, also 19, used to get high and steal cars. Another passenger has been incarcerated repeatedly, an alumnus of Oak Hill Youth Center and the D.C. jail. They are all poor, many of them immigrants or children of immigrants who have fled Central America.

But they are the lucky ones. Tonight, they are riding with Luis.

Cardona roams the streets of Mount Pleasant and Adams-Morgan night after night. He'll collect teenage girls hanging out on street corners and drive them home. He'll give another one a quarter and insist that she check in with her grandmother. He breaks up fights outside clubs and runs interference in disputes between gangs. He'll load up the Pathfinder with "young'uns" and take them to play football or laser tag, to free movie screenings or weekend visits with Piscataway Indians in southern Maryland.

"I'm willing to do whatever it takes to stop these kids from killing each other," he says. "Unfortunately, I don't have much to offer them."

But he does. Cardona, 28, offers them a place to talk, a view of worlds beyond the streets, even a life to emulate.

Charismatic and Controversial

Cardona has emerged as a controversial player in the anti-gang effort in the District's Hispanic neighborhoods. He is a former gang member, albeit one with both a criminal record and a college degree. The organization he works for, Barrios Unidos (United Neighborhoods), was founded with few credentials and almost no money. Its mission is not getting kids out of street gangs, but getting kids on the street to stop committing crimes.

At meetings with the suits from the mayor's office, Cardona wears the street uniform of sneakers, absurdly baggy jeans and oversize sweat shirts. His speech is littered with profanities, and he is frequently disdainful of other youth workers. "The [expletive] I learned on the streets, that's more than a psychiatrist could do," he says. "I deal with psychiatrists who don't know what to do. . . . None of their approaches works. I say, 'Listen, maybe you just should have been a thug.'"

Little wonder, then, that Cardona's critics see him as a hotheaded loudmouth whose bluster far exceeds any genuine impact he may have. They point out that Cardona has no background in psychology, no training in social work or crisis prevention. They are skeptical that he really has gone straight, and Cardona himself echoes their concerns: "There's no guarantee that I'm going to stay on this path for the rest of my life," he says. "I pray for that, but when you work in this kind of environment, with all the stress, you can get caught up, go back to your old ways."

But Cardona has assets as well, most notably his intrusive street-style charisma. The plain fact is that he reaches these kids because he was—and in many ways, still is—one of them.

An Educated Gangster

Cardona's own life is a curious mix of genuine achievement and careless wrongdoing.

Born to a Guatemalan mother and a Puerto Rican father, he grew up in Mount Pleasant, the District's Hispanic enclave. He was raised by his mother, a housecleaner, and his early memories revolve around being angry—about being poor, about not having a father around, about the way his mother would lose her temper when he'd ask for help with his homework. Only years later would he realize that her anger grew from frustration: She couldn't read English.

By the time Cardona was 11, he was breaking into cars, and soon after that he was stealing them. Despite his extracurricular activities, he made it through high school, and not just one of the District's troubled public schools. His mother scrimped to send him to the private St. John's College High School. When he graduated, he was the first in his family to do so.

He enrolled at Howard University the following fall and majored in political science. Still, Cardona kept up his parallel life as a hood, robbing people with his crew. In 1987, he was arrested in Montgomery County, Maryland, on drug distribution charges, for which he was eventually sentenced to three years' probation. He says he was arrested in the District on assault charges as well. Cardona still worries that he owes some debts, that someone he has wronged will retaliate.

It wouldn't be the first time.

A Saturday night in 1991: He was 22 and had downed eight screwdrivers at the Mirage club in Southeast D.C. On the way out, he got into an argument. Dropped the guy to the ground. Kicked him in the head.

Afterward, he and a friend started to drive off but got stuck in traffic. He heard the first gunshot, and saw a dark hole materialize in his friend's neck.

"Then I heard boom-boom-boom-boom-boom," says Cardona. "That [expletive] emptied a 17-round clip in the car." Cardona was hit five times. Both survived.

During the weeks he spent recovering at D.C. General, he contemplated turning his life around. But this wasn't the movies. He wasn't ready.

A Death Brings Inspiration

Eight months later, a close friend was fatally shot inside Adams-Morgan's Kilimanjaro club. At the funeral, his friends plotted retribution, but the man's mother begged them to reconsider. She told them that if they really wanted to honor her son, they should prevent other youths from dying the way he did.

After Cardona graduated from Howard in 1993, he sent out resumes. No one hired him, so he hustled drugs. "Homeboys were like, 'What the [expletive] are you doing?'" He didn't know.

But he kept thinking about what his friend's grieving mother had said. "This is going to sound crazy," he says, "but one afternoon I was riding the bus, and right there on that bus I had divine inspiration. I started having ideas about working with kids. All of a sudden I thought, 'This is what you got to do,' and when I got off the bus I was in tears."

The credentials from his straight life were still good. In the summer of '95, he landed a temporary job as a special projects coordinator for D.C. Delegate Eleanor Holmes Norton.

One afternoon that fall, he collected some of the younger neighborhood kids, piled them in his Pathfinder and took them to the Georgetown University campus to play football. That was the genesis of an organization he immodestly dubbed the Foundation for Youth at Risk. "It was no more than me riding around in my truck, picking up these homeboys and taking them to go play football at Georgetown and Howard University," he says. "I was trying to get them away from the neighborhood. . . .

"I loved it. It felt like being in my gang all over again. The fun, everybody . . . jonin' on one another. . . . I was like, 'Hey look, let's do what y'all want to do, anything other than getting high or getting drunk or doing something illegal.'

"They used to always say, 'Come on man, let's get [expletive] up.' I'd say, 'Uh-uh, man. That's not my style.'"

Meeting Kids Halfway

Barrios Unidos's regular Monday night meetings always begin with the burning of sage. Two dozen teenagers and a handful of adults sit in a circle of chairs in the library of the *Sojourners* magazine offices on 15th Street NW. They rise and clasp hands. Cardona places the dried herb in an ashtray, lights it, then blows out the flame. As the ashtray passes from hand to hand, each person leans forward and fans the smoke toward face and chest.

Despite the solemnity of the opening ritual, the meetings tend to be informal, even chaotic. Occasionally a guest speaker will join the group, but mostly the kids just talk. They talk about what they did over the weekend, about neighborhood gang feuds, about who has been skipping school and why.

"The meetings are pretty damn near the only opportunity these young people have to be in a family-type environment," Cardona says. "These kids have no sense of belonging, whether it be in their families, their schools, the job force—whatever. In the meetings, we create a community around them."

It is a relatively small community. Cardona lectures to school assemblies and occasionally travels across town to work with kids whose street alliances make them unwelcome in Adams-Morgan and Mount Pleasant. But he devotes most of his time to an ever-shifting group of approximately 30 kids.

By contrast, the Latin American Youth Center, the most established organization working with young Hispanics in Washington, helps approximately 5,000 youngsters and their families each year. The center has been operating in Mount Pleasant for 25 years and has an annual budget of $2.9 million.

In 1995, D.C. Barrios Unidos's start-up budget was $7,000, say board members. The 1996 figure was higher—$30,000—but the board could afford to pay Cardona's $26,000 annual salary for only eight months. "To him," says board secretary Aaron Gallegos, "it doesn't really matter whether he gets paid or not. He's made it clear to the board that he's going to work with the kids anyway."

A Grass-Roots Movement

Barrios Unidos was founded in the late '70s in Santa Cruz, California, by a group of ex-cons who had watched their neighborhoods disintegrate into what national director Daniel "Nane" Alejandrez calls "the madness." A nonprofit organization that gets most of its funding from foundation grants, Barrios Unidos now has 27 chapters, all fueled by a philosophy encompassing a grass-roots anti-violence ethic and Latinos' "cultural reconnection" to their heritage.

"We see this as a spiritual movement," Alejandrez says. "How else can you continue to work in this madness, burying young people . . . and still stay sane, still have that hope?"

When Cardona first approached Barrios Unidos about starting a D.C. chapter (there is also one in Fairfax County, Virginia), Alejandrez was dubious. But it wasn't long, he says, before he was impressed by Cardona's energy, commitment and grasp of street concepts of honor and respect. "He knew that there was a protocol," Alejandrez says.

But not everyone approves of Cardona's approach, and it is precisely his street ways that so gall his critics. Other youth workers criticize Cardona only under the cloak of anonymity, because they don't want to be perceived by the Hispanic community, or the foundations who fund them, as disparaging someone trying to do good work.

"Is being out on the streets at 3 or 4 at night an effective youth worker strategy?" a detractor asks. "Is that a solid prevention technique?"

Board member Gallegos defends Cardona's late-night cruising. "From our perspective, that's exactly what needs to be done. It's like the parable of the lost sheep. The shepherd goes after the lost sheep," he says. "Nobody else is doing that."

"We don't get a very good reputation because people see Luis out at all hours of the night. They look at this image and the kind of car he drives and always having the kids hanging out with him," Gallegos says. "The kids see him as one of them, and also as somebody who has put his own life on the line for them. He goes to bat for them. He advocates for them with police, teachers, community organizations."

Cardona's champions include Bell Multicultural High School Principal Maria Tukeva, who has asked some of the Barrios Unidos kids at

Bell to approach other students she thought could benefit from the program. "I've seen improvement in attendance . . . behavior . . . more interest and motivation to complete schoolwork," she says. "In probably 90 percent of the cases I've seen that.

"There's something about the philosophy of the organization and the way Luis relates directly to them on their level and holds them to high expectations," she adds. "They've been able to accept him as a kind of authority figure, and they may have had a hard time accepting anyone else as an authority figure."

Jose Robert Magana, a District police officer who also grew up in Mount Pleasant and knew Cardona in the bad old days, says he is effective with troubled Hispanic teenagers because he shares their experiences. "The trouble that Luis has been in and these kids have been in is somewhat similar," Magana says. "I don't want to say he comes down to their level, but he sort of meets them halfway."

The Birth and Salvation of a Gangster

Julio Somoza used to dream about living in the United States. "Everyone said life is different in America; there's no war, no death squads," he says.

When he was 12, his mother, who had left El Salvador eight years earlier to wait tables in Alexandria, could finally afford to bring him to the United States.

He arrived expecting "something like Disneyland." But at Thomas Jefferson Middle School in Arlington, Virginia, his classmates tormented him. They called him "amigo" and told him to go back to his country. Even the other Latinos looked down on him—their English was better.

Soon, the teasing turned into brawls, but by then Somoza had befriended other Spanish-speaking students. "There was a lot of us being attacked by African American and Vietnamese gangs. We decided to group together for a common purpose, self-defense," he says. "As soon as we grouped together, we had some kind of power."

Somoza was expected to help support his family, and when the combination of his high school classes and full-time job became too oppressive, he says, "I started slinging [selling] weed, started dealing to make some money and help my mom." He says he also began drinking and using cocaine, and that he stole stereos to support his habit.

One night, he was hanging downtown with his crew when Cardona rolled up. They eyed him warily. "He comes over to the table and he starts talking about Barrios Unidos and peace and unity and brotherhood," says Somoza. "Everyone is like, 'What's with this guy? He smoking the chronic [marijuana]?' But I was feeling kind of funny. Right there and then, I felt like a piece of my puzzle had come to [a] place inside me.

"I needed the guidance," says Somoza, now 21 and working full time as an electrician's apprentice. "He's given me so much knowledge. Taught me to read about my history and background. I'm a descendant of the Mayan people. Nobody can get me mad now if they call me a foreigner. I can just look at them and laugh and say, 'Hey man, you the foreigner.'"

Outreach in the Midst of Madness

Many of the Barrios Unidos kids receive scant attention from their parents, who are struggling to adjust to life in a new country. This may have something to do with their affection for the perpetually available Cardona.

But affection doesn't necessarily change behavior.

Another Barrios Unidos kid, a slight young man with an unruly Afro, doesn't want his name used in this story because he still sells drugs.

He grew up hard in Brooklyn, where he had three brothers. They're all dead. At 19, he's convinced that he, too, will die on the street. A large cross is tattooed on his back, stretching from just below the nape of his neck to the red underpants that peek out above his baggy jeans. "Perdon Madre," it reads. Forgive me Mother.

Sometimes, he imagines a regular life—a house maybe, a kid. He could be a veterinarian. But he's not entirely sure about that.

"The streets is like a drug, for real. It's like dope. You need to be on the streets to feel better," he says. "I want to change but I really don't. . . . I know what I want, but I don't know if I can accomplish it."

He's going to try. "When I got locked up last time, I thought about how Luis was going to get mad. I let him down. He's helping us to go one way, and we go the other way. Luis is a warrior. He doing a lot of things a lot of those outreach workers wouldn't do.

"We look at him as a true hustler," he says. "He got his education, then he changed."

Finding Hope in Education

At a Monday meeting, the guest speaker is a sober young Latino from the University of Maryland's financial aid office. He passes out literature about loans and work-study programs, then gives an earnest, encouraging speech.

A debate on the merits of college follows.

One board member points out that only 5 percent of Latinos across the country attend college. She explains how her college degree helped her get her job. The kids argue that if you work in construction, you earn money right away. And if you can make your way up to a management position at McDonald's, you could make $7 an hour.

Jose Marquez, who says he's thinking about getting a high school equivalency diploma, raises his hand. "If you get a loan and you don't pay them back, do they send a repo man after you?" Everyone laughs.

Someone else says he would just take the money and run—back to El Salvador. The meeting starts to disintegrate. One kid leans over and punches another in the gut.

Cardona looks embarrassed. "Yo! Yo man, let's show some respect. Yo, when I was your age, I was joking around about college, too," he says. "Y'all are closer to college than you think. . . . You got a lot of talent and a lot of brains. Think about what you could do with a degree."

The debate resumes. Attuned to the circumstances of his charges, Cardona raises a question no one else will ask:

"Is it true that if you get a felony arrest for distribution of drugs that your state won't give you money for school?"

Paying a Debt

Another night. Cardona takes a small group to El Faro, an Adams-Morgan restaurant. The boys are cutting up, using their menus as weapons.

Luis picks up a copy of *El Pregonero*, a local Spanish-language weekly, and starts reading a list of Latinos who've been killed in the area recently.

The roughhousing stops, and the boys look at Cardona intently.

"They forgot Flaco," one murmurs softly.

"And Giovanni, too," says another.

"Yeah," says Cardona.

For a long while, no one says anything.

Cardona is haunted by the kids he couldn't save. "The ones I dealt with on a peripheral level," he says. "I always feel like if I had gotten them into the programs, a lot of them would still be alive."

When Cardona gets frustrated, he broods about his own circumstances. He barely has time for a social life. Money is so tight he's had to move back in with his mother.

"I'm [expletive] dealing with everybody else's pain and and I'm not even dealing with my own," he says. "I'm still thinking about what it's like to not have a daddy around, to almost die. I'm dealing with all the pain I put my mom through."

But his soul-searching always comes back to this: "I figure this is my way of paying back for the things I've done," he says.

In June of 1997, almost a dozen of Cardona's kids will graduate from high school, and two have been accepted to college. He's proud of their achievement, but he also finds the prospect daunting.

"All I was trying to do was make sure they didn't kill themselves," he says.

That's a lot, actually. After so many nights of driving around his neighborhood, maybe he finally got somewhere.

MOTHERS AGAINST GANGS

Laura Laughlin

Mothers Against Gangs is a national nonprofit organization dedicated to the prevention of gang violence and activity. In the following selection, *Phoenix New Times* reporter Laura Laughlin recounts the formation of the first chapter of Mothers Against Gangs in Phoenix, Arizona. As she explains, Sophia Lopez-Espindola started the chapter after the death of her teenage son, who was caught in the crossfire between two rival gangs in January 1992. Over time, Laughlin writes, the Phoenix chapter has developed a number of intervention and prevention techniques designed to steer the area's young people away from gangs. She describes the various services offered by the organization, including after-school activities for children and teens, tutoring, career information, grief support groups, and discussion sessions.

The story of the Phoenix chapter of Mothers Against Gangs—how it began, how it has evolved and survived over the years—begins with a 3 A.M. knock on a patio door.

It was the type of summons every parent dreads, a startling middle-of-the-night announcement that a child has been hurt. Sophia Lopez and her husband headed to St. Joseph's Hospital and Medical Center, hoping that their son, Edward, hadn't been seriously injured.

They found him lying peacefully in a hospital bed. He was sitting up, his hands folded over his chest. A small bandage on the left side of his forehead hid a clean entrance wound where a bullet had pierced his brain and effectively ended his life. He was breathing with the help of a respirator.

Edward Joe Anthony Lopez, a good kid and an accomplished athlete, had been shot in the crossfire of a battle between two gangs. He died about 5 A.M. on January 5, 1992, two hours after his life-support system was disconnected.

A Tragedy Breeds Action

It was a quiet finish to the life of the 16-year-old Tolleson High School student. But it prompted his mother to start making noise. Shocked and confused by the death of a son she believed had no ties to gangs,

Excerpted from "One Tough Mother," by Laura Laughlin, *Phoenix New Times*, November 18, 1999. Copyright © 1999 by *Phoenix New Times*. Reprinted with permission.

Lopez began making phone calls and writing letters, seeking meetings, answers, help. She asked about the details of the shooting, criti-
cized police handling of the case, fumed at a society that offered no
support for parents like herself, argued against the decision not to
prosecute the youth who shot Edward. She also asked what could be
done to stop the gang violence in the Phoenix area.

Her quest for answers led her to start a chapter of Mothers Against
Gangs—based on a similar organization in Chicago. Years after starting
Mothers Against Gangs, Lopez, who now goes by Lopez-Espindola, continues her efforts to end gang violence. But while her mission is the
same, her methods as well as the structure and membership of her
group have changed dramatically over the years.

In a journey Lopez-Espindola calls "pretty rocky," she has enjoyed
attention and accolades, but has also weathered disappointments,
gunshots, even a criminal conviction for election fraud. The group
has grown from a tiny, self-financed operation run out of Lopez-
Espindola's Maryvale home to an organization with its own center, a
paid staff of seven, a volunteer pool of about 200 people and an
annual budget of $326,000.

The nonprofit program, funded by donations and grants, recently
scored big when it was selected by Save the Children, a 75-year-old
international aid organization, as one of eight urban centers to participate in a $20 million national effort to increase the availability and
quality of after-school options for children. Save the Children leaders
say they see a successful formula for helping kids in Mothers Against
Gangs. It's a partnership that will translate into at least $150,000 in
cash and in-kind services for Lopez-Espindola's group.

And despite the name, mothers aren't really the driving force
behind the organization anymore. Instead, kids are helping kids. And
they're making a difference.

A Young Volunteer

For six years, Jennie Palomo spent much of her time behind the center's reception desk. She found her way there when she was a 17-year-
old runaway and high school dropout.

Her mother abandoned Palomo and her four siblings when she was
7 years old. The oldest, she had taken on adult responsibilities at an
early age, helping her father raise the younger children. Her father
battled alcoholism, her aunt—a sort of surrogate mother—had died.

An honor student in high school, Palomo says she wasn't officially
in a gang, but all her friends were. She was involved in drugs and alcohol, although not heavily. She wanted to get away from her house, to
be on her own, but she didn't know what to do with herself. So when
Lopez-Espindola's daughter Venus (a friend of Palomo's brother) suggested she come down to the Mothers Against Gangs center, she did.
She would hang out, answer phones and shadow Lopez-Espindola.

"She was the only one working at the center at the time, so whenever she left, she would actually have to shut down the center. And she would take me and another guy along with her to meetings and schools," Palomo says.

Slowly, Palomo got interested in the work the organization did. She began to volunteer, helping run grief support groups for kids. She says a lot of adult volunteers and staffers would leave after a short stint, so kids were getting disillusioned. Having kids work with other kids is a more effective way of getting through to them, she believes.

Palomo says Lopez-Espindola helped her get into a charter school, where she obtained her high school diploma. She got a scholarship to Phoenix College, which she now attends in addition to working a new job at a bank. She plans to go to law school someday and would like to live in New York.

Without Lopez-Espindola and Mothers Against Gangs, Palomo says, "I can't imagine where I would be. I'd be lost."

And without Palomo, the organization might not be where it is today.

Palomo began helping Lopez-Espindola with grant proposals. "I type faster than Sophia does, so I just started helping her fill out the forms. And I would edit them while I did it."

Where other paid grant writers failed to secure funding for Mothers Against Gangs, Palomo succeeded. She says because she had been through the center's programs, she was better able to explain them on the applications. And, she says, officials were impressed with her own story when she made personal presentations at corporations and elsewhere.

Palomo's work produced more than $400,000 in grants, including awards from Save the Children, the Arizona Department of Public Safety, the Community Development Block Grant program, the Phoenix Suns and the Arizona Diamondbacks, the Gannett Corp and Value Options.

The organization doesn't have studies or statistics to demonstrate its success. It says it has served more than 45,000 kids between 1994 and 1999, most of them male and Hispanic. But the group has no way of proving how many kids it has kept out of gangs or how many lives it has turned around.

Still, Lopez-Espindola can tell many tales of troubled kids who have turned successful. And real-life examples of reformed lives can be found merely by visiting the center.

Jose Oromi of Save the Children puts it this way: "They are saving lives."

A Haven for At-Risk Youth

It's easy to drive by the Mothers Against Gangs center without noticing it. At 1401 East Thomas, just down the street from the Phoenix Country Club and North High School, the converted fire station sits on a corner where traffic whizzes by.

The little building is a monument to the type of work that goes on there. Bright, colorful murals depicting a mother and child, kids holding hands and lots of flowers adorn the outside walls. A blob of paint on what used to be the fire station's garage door masks some graffiti. Outside the front door, large copies of "The Golden Rules" are posted in Spanish and English. They dictate peaceful, respectful behavior, outlaw gang colors, drugs, tobacco and alcohol and declare the center "a neutral zone."

Throughout the facility, on the outdoor playgrounds and the indoor recreation room, on the computers, in the kitchen, sitting on worn-out chairs and behind desks, are kids. From 9 A.M. to 7 P.M., they stream in and out. Little ones, some of whom have been going there since they were toddlers, paint pictures, play Nintendo on a prehistoric-looking video-game monitor, work on their homework with older kids. Adolescents and teenagers play pool or foosball, listen to music, hang out with the younger ones and help clean up. Others answer phones, compose letters on computers and send faxes announcing upcoming events.

Most of the center's employees and many of its volunteers are young people who used to be in trouble, came to the center for help and stayed around to help others. One North High student, Dustin Kornelussen, 16, started coming by just for something to do after school. He says he's never been in trouble, but his work at the center may help keep him out. He has signed on as a volunteer, playing with the younger visitors, helping them with their homework.

Inspired to Lead

Lopez-Espindola says kids are the ones who really run the place now. They have painted the walls inside and out, drawn the artwork and laid the carpet and tile. They help in case management, event planning, grant writing. And they lead support groups for kids in gangs.

The weekly gatherings, kind of a cross between peer therapy and support groups, were the idea of Rudy Lopez, Edward's younger brother. Rudy, who was involved in gangs back when Edward was killed, according to his mother, proposed that in addition to the grieving support group for parents, she start a similar group for kids.

Over the years, more structured sessions have developed, with a broader range of discussion topics. Initially led by Rudy, and later by other young volunteers, the evening groups consist of 12- or 20-week sessions with a curriculum that covers topics ranging from self-esteem to grief to domestic violence and sexual behavior. Lopez-Espindola and police officers sometimes sit in.

The courts and other institutions have put the Mothers Against Gangs program to work for them, too. The sessions are sometimes required as community-service hours, either as a condition of probation or to help earn free tattoo removal from the Phoenix Parks and Recreation Department.

Kids meet for hourly sessions once or twice a week and must first watch a video depicting the death of Edward Lopez and the birth of Mothers Against Gangs.

In October 1999, Save the Children commissioned a study of the youth program—the only evaluation ever done of a Mothers Against Gangs program. The review looked at only a small group of kids in one of the 20-week sessions. But it suggested that the youth groups were helping the kids because 90 percent of the young people had learned, among other things, how to better control their anger and to consider consequences of their actions. . . .

Frank Garcia is a former gang member who now works for Mothers Against Gangs. He tells the group members, most of them slumping in their chairs, that he envies them because they have a chance to avoid the same gang life he chose.

"You should get a job, get a house, get a family, be happy," he says.

Before the next group session the following week, Jose Beltran says he was struck by Garcia's messages.

"He knows what's up, he knows what he's saying," says Beltran, who is on house arrest and must come to the center to perform more than 200 hours of community service.

Teens in Trouble

A skinny 16-year-old who wears an electronic monitoring bracelet on his right ankle and a woeful expression on his face, Beltran has been to Mothers Against Gangs before. In 1997, he was picked up for a weapons violation and was ordered to serve 200 hours at the center. He didn't go through the youth program then, because he couldn't fit it in with his work schedule.

Lopez-Espindola says Beltran and his cousins came to the center together then and made progress. But once they were back home and on the streets, she says, they began to get into trouble again.

Beltran's latest arrest came when a group of kids started shooting at him and some girls in a car. He says he drove home, got his gun, returned and fired back. Now he is allowed to go only to work or to the Mothers Against Gangs center. If his monitor goes off once, he'll face a stiff penalty, either being held in custody until he's 18 or transferred to adult court.

He tells the group he wants to change his ways. "But it's not as easy as that. I'm trying to stay out of trouble, [but] I'm not going to just be kicking back when people keep messing with me. They keep messing with me."

Beltran says his enemies keep taunting him. They even broke his car window recently and he was powerless to retaliate. "I can't even go out of my yard," he says.

When he describes the crime that got him back into trouble, Garcia stops him when he talks about going home to retrieve his weapon. That, he says, is where Beltran could have avoided arrest. He should have stayed away.

The bright light in his life, Beltran says, is the daughter he fathered when he was 14. Having her has made him want to "start calming down," he says, because he doesn't want her to get hurt or grow up without knowing her father. And while Beltran's own mother has told him to consider moving to get away from the gangs, he wants to stay and watch his daughter grow up.

"She's just starting to say, 'Daddy,'" he says. But he says her mother won't let him see the child, a situation he's trying to change.

This is something else Frank Garcia can relate to. He tells Beltran he has a son from a prior relationship, but the mother won't let him see the boy because of his gangster past.

"It hurts, it hurts deeply inside," he says.

"*Mejor* [better] to beat you up a whole bunch of times," the teenager replies.

All of the teenagers in this group are here because they have committed crimes. Some of them are involved in gangs, others aren't. They say kids join gangs because they want to feel protected and be popular. When asked to define a gang, one boy says it's people trying to protect a neighborhood, another says it's a group trying to be better than anyone else. Beltran says a gang is a group of guys that hang out. As to what a victim is, a 15-year-old offender offers: "A person that gets hurt that wasn't supposed to."

George Acedo, a 17-year-old dropout, is at the center performing 60 hours of service after a burglary arrest. He says that staying in a gang will land you in "a tomb, a hospital or jail." He has asked Garcia how he can remove the gang symbols from his remote-controlled race car.

Frank Garcia tells the teenagers that if he can get out of the gang life, they can, too. "I walked away and I feel proud that I walked away. You know why? Because I'm not getting locked up. I'm not killing anybody. I'm not getting killed. . . . I know how you feel. I don't go out. I don't go to clubs. I don't want to get shot at. I know it's hard out there because I've been there."

A Gangster Background

Looking at Frank Garcia today, it's hard to imagine him as a gangster.

He is 27 years old, with a baby face. When he comes to work at Mothers Against Gangs, he is clean-cut, neatly dressed. Even his white tee shirts are pressed. He welcomes visitors (no matter how many times he has met them) with a firm handshake, a huge smile and a warm greeting.

But he says, not long ago, "you wouldn't have liked me." He was a banger who looked and acted the part. A member of Las Cuatro Milpas—one of the oldest gangs in Phoenix—since he was 11 or 12, Garcia fulfilled all his obligations to the gang. He used and dealt drugs. He has arrests for robbery, burglary, vehicle theft and other minor incidents on his juvenile record. When he and some buddies broke into a Montgomery Ward and stole $4,000 worth of equipment, Garcia was sent to adult court where he squandered a break by violating his probation. When he was 19, he made the news after he and a teenager got into a dispute with a stranger at a gas station, then chased him through the streets of Phoenix in their car, firing shots at him.

Garcia says it wasn't until well after he had served about a year and a half in jail and prison that he decided to quit the gangster life. And when he did, he just severed his ties. He didn't move out of his old neighborhood, but he quit seeing his friends, didn't answer their phone calls, didn't invite them to his wedding.

He says this really wasn't as hard as it sounds, because a lot of his old friends are dead or in prison. While his wife is worried that others may seek him out and retaliate for leaving the gang, Garcia says he's not afraid.

"I ain't scared of nobody because I'm my own man. I'm gonna live my own life, without people telling me what to do and who to hang out with," he says.

Steps Toward Reform

When he got out of prison, he found it hard to get jobs with a felony on his record. Once, when he withheld that information on his application, he got hired for a warehouse position. He claims he was doing well until he was called into a supervisor's office and let go because of his deception.

"My heart just dropped," he says. "I went home and cried my heart out. It was like I was trying and I couldn't get anywhere."

He had gotten another job at the Bashas' distribution center, but hadn't started working there, when he began volunteering at Mothers Against Gangs a few months ago. When Lopez-Espindola realized his work schedule would cut into time with kids, she offered him a paid position.

Garcia says he is grateful that older gang members he met in prison advised him to quit the life before he ended up spending the rest of his days behind bars. He says he regrets all the pain he has caused his family, but he is thankful to his mother for encouraging him when he was in trouble and paying for a good lawyer to represent him.

"My mom's real proud of me now. She's just telling me to do what makes me happy. And this makes me happy," he says.

He takes a yellow sticky note and draws a line from right to left. As he dips the line down in the middle, Garcia says that was the trap of the gang life for him. He draws another parallel line, this one with an upward arc in the middle.

"I want to show kids there is a way around gangs, a detour around what I did," he says.

A Pragmatic Approach

For someone whose son was cut down by a gang member, Lopez-Espindola is surprisingly compassionate toward the gangsters who come by the center.

"We have so much respect from the gangs because they know we are not against them," she says. "We are against the crimes they are committing. We don't see them as gang members. We see them as kids. And we will do anything we can to help them. But once they cross the line, we'll prosecute them to the fullest."

Lopez-Espindola believes that when it comes to gang involvement, both prevention and intervention can be effective. She thinks prevention techniques should start as early as kindergarten, because children in troubled families are exposed to drugs and violence at young ages. She cites an example of a 4-year-old boy who used to sit on the roof of a nearby apartment complex, acting as a lookout for his drug-addicted mother. By the time he moved away, she says, he was flashing gang signs. While some say intervention is nearly impossible—once a gangster, always a gangster—Lopez-Espindola disagrees.

"It's never too late," she says. She constantly preaches the value of self-worth, advising adults and children alike to look at their mistakes as lessons from which they can learn and move on.

Lopez-Espindola has snapshots and school pictures from kids who have been through the center, have stayed out of trouble and have kept in touch. One third-grader was referred to the center from a school principal after he stabbed a kindergartner. He's now in high school and is doing well, Lopez-Espindola reports.

Another alumna of the center graduated recently from Project Challenge, a state-funded boot camp for kids in trouble. When asked to select a mentor to help him on his road to success, he chose Lopez-Espindola. He's clean-cut, doing well and planning to attend college after he joins the service, she says.

Other former gangbangers give testimonials at celebrations like the September anniversary party thrown at the center. Several speakers paid homage to Lopez-Espindola for helping change their lives and to the center for providing a safe place for them and others.

An Array of Services

The center does more than provide security and lectures on the perils of gangbanging.

Families can come to the center for almost any type of help. They can get assistance planning and paying for funerals. They can find out how to tell if children are in gangs or hate groups and what to do if they are. Information is available on careers, health and safety. Caseworkers refer them to proper agencies.

Probation officers have regular hours there. And Mothers Against Gangs feeds needy visitors, ordering pizza daily for the children who often stay until dinnertime, offering free food at special events, serving leftovers later to families in the neighborhood.

Students who have been suspended or expelled from school come by the center, spending days there working on schoolwork, getting tutored or performing office work rather than languishing at home or on the streets.

Mothers Against Gangs also works with Call-A-Teen, the charter school at 649 North Sixth Avenue. Lopez-Espindola, who has sent her own children there, says at-risk kids can get a second chance there without being labeled or judged.

Principal Gloria Junkersfeld says the school accepts the types of students other schools have kicked out or given up on, tailoring coursework and schedules to help them succeed. The half-day curriculum, six-week courses and open enrollment policies make the school a perfect place for the dropouts and troubled youngsters whom Lopez-Espindola encounters.

Other districts and schools also cooperate with the center. Rick Cohen, who directs a program at Loma Linda Elementary School called Students With Authority to Teach, says he and Lopez-Espindola have a tag-team approach to helping kids. His program for students in grades four through eight aims to teach children problem-solving skills as they encounter violence, drugs and gangs in their area. Those children then reach out to other kids, he says, much in the same way the volunteers at Mothers Against Gangs help their peers.

Reaching the Young Children

The younger children who visit the Thomas Street center don't wax philosophical against gangs and violence when asked why they come there. They just say it's fun, then talk about eating pizza, playing games and working on computers. Some of them say they come every day after school for help on their homework. Many of them say their parents aren't home anyway. And while they are swinging and playing and hanging out, they seem to be getting the message to stay away from gangs.

Erik Stewart, 8, who has been coming to the center since he was 3, says even though he recently moved to South Phoenix, his mom drives him to his old school so he can continue going to Mothers Against Gangs. He says he knows some kids in gangs but he plans to stay away "'cause you can get into trouble and my mom could take away my allowance."

Another 8-year-old boy playing Nintendo one afternoon says he wants to become a police officer. He says he has older brothers and a sister who don't come to the center. And he doesn't really try to pass on what he's learned about staying out of trouble.

"No, they like gangs," he says.

Michael Mora, 10, has turned his life around at an early age. His mother says she began to get worried when she noticed Michael dressing and talking like a gangster, drawing pictures of low-rider cars and practicing Old English graffiti-style lettering. He would brag to his elementary school friends that his cousins were in gangs. When Michael was in third grade, he colored a leprechaun for a class assignment. Elena Mora was horrified when he brought it home.

"He had drawn eight-balls for buttons on the shirt, Nike symbols on his shoes, a gun in one hand and a knife in the other," she says.

When she went to the principal, he advised her not to worry. But Mora decided to take action. She enrolled Michael in a charter school, left her full-time job for part-time paralegal work and contacted Lopez-Espindola.

Now Michael and his mom both volunteer for Mothers Against Gangs. Each weekday, Mora gets off work, picks up Michael at school and heads for the center. Michael, dressed neatly in his school uniform, a navy golf shirt and khaki shorts, always stops in at Lopez-Espindola's office for a bear hug. His mom says he is interested in sports for the first time and has quit mimicking and admiring gang members.

"I've seen a total change," says Elena Mora.

Michael, a red and yellow sucker in his mouth, says he used to see drugs and gang activity at his old school. "That needs to stop," he says.

Later, he apologizes. "I shouldn't have spoken with a sucker in my mouth. That was rude."

Staying True to Her Course

Mothers Against Gangs has had its ups and downs. Heartened initially by support from mothers and others in the community, Lopez-Espindola says she has been disappointed by many people. Charley Ruiz, a member of the state's G.I.T.E.M. [Gang Intelligence and Team Enforcement Mission] anti-gang task force who has supported Mothers Against Gangs since its inception, credits Lopez-Espindola with remaining true to her goal, despite some problems, political turmoil and troubled alliances.

Trained as a cosmetologist, Lopez-Espindola has had to teach herself practically everything about running a nonprofit organization. She says some board members and others didn't follow through on their commitment to the organization. One former board member that she considered a mentor mishandled finances at another nonprofit group. Another volunteer took grant-writing materials to get an education grant for herself.

There have been break-ins, thefts from the center, bullets fired into her office. Neighbors have blamed kids from the center for graffiti and other problems.

But Lopez-Espindola has continued her mission. . . .

Over the years, she has forged alliances with the Phoenix Police Department, the Department of Public Safety, the Latino Peace Officers Association, neighborhood groups and city officials. She has been supported by businesses including Motorola, Honeywell, Arizona Public Service Company (APS) and Bashas'. And the city provided a huge boost in 1993 when it let the organization take over the abandoned fire station on Thomas Road, charging $1 a year rent.

"The people that I've come across at the center, I'm really impressed with their own sense of purpose and their own initiative to get involved," says Rick Cohen of Loma Linda Elementary School. "Sophia has been an inspiration for me. She has empowered kids to make their own decisions and get involved in their own way. You can have a strong leader and make them follow you. But you are just a figurehead. And when you take that figurehead away, you've got nothing."

INTERVENTION METHODS FOR GANG GIRLS: SPECIAL CONSIDERATIONS

Mark S. Fleisher

Mark S. Fleisher is a professor of criminal justice at Illinois State University in Normal. Beginning in 1994, Fleisher undertook an extended study of the teenage members of Kansas City's Fremont Hustlers gang; his research formed the basis for his book *Dead End Kids: Gang Girls and the Boys They Know*, from which the following excerpt is taken. According to the author, gang girls require special intervention techniques, primarily because they often have babies or toddlers to care for. Intervention methods that do not take into account the need of gang girls for childcare, safe housing, and vocational and social training will not be effective, he concludes.

My Fremont research shows that a youth gang's social life is an intricate set of economic transactions which have social effects. The underlying socioeconomic principle is this: When kids perceive a gain by doing one thing instead of another, they move in the direction of the gain. When there's a perception of greater gain in selling drugs than in doing school work, drug selling wins. The principle operates in purely social transactions. When there's greater gain in hanging out with a gang than in avoiding it, the gang wins. When a girl perceives greater gain in having a relationship with an abusive boy than in having no boyfriend, there's victimization of teenage girls.

Likewise, delinquency and gang intervention can operate on the same socioeconomic principle of gain. Generally speaking, youth-gang intervention is a struggle over money: gang kids earn cash by selling high-profit drugs like rock cocaine, all the while that hundreds of millions of dollars are spent by federal, state, and local crime-control agencies to suppress or prevent gang-related drug selling and other crimes linked to gangs.

The dynamic process central to gang intervention is like tug-of-war: communities must convince gang kids that there's greater long-term gain in sticking with an "eight-to-five," usually blue-collar, low-wage, shift-work job, which they don't want to do, than in continuing a rela-

Excerpted from *Dead End Kids: Gang Girls and the Boys They Know*, by Mark S. Fleisher (Madison, WI: The University of Wisconsin Press, 1998). Reprinted with permission.

tively easy, albeit risky, drug-selling–hanging-out lifestyle.

If kids gradually accept this economic shift, they'll eventually acquire a sense of the underlying philosophical and moral shift in lifestyle orientations. Gang life is predicated on immediate economic gain from drug and other crime profits and social gain from the agency of rulelessness. Mainstream life is oriented toward the future, and social and material gains are slower but steadier, more reliable, and less risky.

The irony is that communities have more to lose than gang kids do in failed intervention and a great deal more to gain in successful intervention. If communities can convince gang kids to trade a profitable unlawful job for a less-profitable lawful one, then the community expenses attached to gang crime (drug selling, burglary, carjacking) and gang-related social problems (child abuse and neglect, drug addiction, teenage pregnancy, truancy and dropping out of school) will diminish gradually for the majority of community members as gang members pull away from the street and lead their children toward mainstream lifestyles.

Encouraging a Shift in Priorities

The unlawful-to-lawful shift in income production and the social changes it effects over multiple generations are what I mean by *youth-gang intervention*. This is a difficult shift to encourage and even more difficult to accomplish. Fremont research shows that gang kids do engage in this economic transition even on their own, and that doing so results in less crime and less serious crime. . . .

Successful gang intervention depends on offering gang kids the unlawful-to-lawful socioeconomic trade by showing them exactly what they have to gain. Some community members may feel this is "coddling young criminals." But remember that taxpayers fund intervention and crime-control policies, and they have the most to gain and to lose. The truth is, without the consensus of gang kids, gang and delinquency intervention always loses, crime soars, costs skyrocket.

Legislators and community officials who hurl threats at gang kids will get only a sore throat. Gang kids aren't moved by preaching or screaming. Cara [one of the Fremont gang girls] too is a hard sell. She saw no immediate benefit in an education and a GED, so she quit. She had a job at Taco Bell, and a GED wouldn't have added one cent to her income. Like most teenagers, Cara didn't connect more education today with economic gain in the year 2005. What's more, Fremont kids are too cynical to believe that history and algebra lessons will ensure a "better tomorrow." Even my college students don't believe that.

What moves gang kids to act? The answer is simple: immediate material gain, including money, food, clothes, and shelter. Improvements these kids can see, touch, and possess will pull them off the street. Only after they are sheltered and protected will most of them pay attention to less tangible aspects of their lives. These kids aren't stupid; they know when they're better off in one situation than in another. The trick is to involve them socially and emotionally in their own intervention to the same degree they have been involved in their own destruction.

Community mobilization and a carefully designed system that, first, improves the quality of life and, second, integrates that improvement with educational and vocational training can help remedy the effects of social and economic poverty.

Gang-Girl Intervention

I advocate the implementation of supervised residential centers designed for gang girls. Gang boys shouldn't be overlooked, but their intervention can be simpler than girls', and more delinquent and gang boys are already exposed to intervention.

In 1995, 74 percent of juveniles arrested were boys under age 18. While in detention centers and jail, these offenders receive social, psychological, and educational and vocational services. If young men are exposed to such programs and subsequently choose gang life over straight life, then America's culture of personal choice should let these young adults accept the responsibility of that choice.

True, a culture of choice is open to girls too, but gang girls pose a special intervention obstacle: babies. Many gang girls have preschool children. Doing little more than classroom education has no immediate material effect on their lives and doesn't improve their children's lives either. In short, inadequate intervention for gang-girl mothers and their children has a high opportunity cost. If communities focus on gang boys and ignore gang-girl mothers, their children are likely to reside in dysfunctional homes [where gang life is the norm]. If police arrest gang-girl mothers and imprison them, who will care for their children and what will be the conditions of care?

Gang-girl intervention is crime control. Pulling gang girls off the street may, over time, weaken the fluid residential pattern of gang boys and, at the same time, stabilize female-headed households. Many of the Fremont gang girls provided a stable residential system which gang boys used to sustain a drug-selling street lifestyle.

Fremont research shows that a baby is an effective link between its mother and father only when the father perceives some material benefit from such an attachment. . . . As long as the mothers of the children of gang boys have apartments and houses, these boys will have a place to hang out and sell drugs. . . .

Breaking the Pattern

To ensure that these girls and their children are safe, communities must encourage them to leave the street. One thing is certain: communities should never count on gang boys to assist their pregnant girlfriends or their babies' mothers. Encouraging girls to abandon the street will disrupt boys' residential patterns, protect girls from abuse and another pregnancy, and shelter gang girls' children.

Fremont research also shows that gang girls neglect their children either because of apathy engendered by drug addiction or because of a lack of resources to provide a safe environment. When these young children are neglected for any reason, they end up sitting in [a gang girl's] apartment, breathing cigarette and marijuana smoke, listening to gangster rap, and surrounded by young gangsters.

The intervention option with the lowest long-term cost is to locate young gang-affiliated mothers somewhere that they can be given options that increase their gain and protect their children. Let's remember that we're focusing on adolescents who are 14 to 17 years old; kids this age don't plan well for the future and have no realistic idea about social and economic issues embedded in rearing children.

Finding young mothers and teenagers like Cara, who may not be pregnant today but will be tomorrow, might be the most difficult challenge of an intervention program that targets teenage girls and young mothers and their children. This subpopulation is hidden inside youth gangs, and we're unsure about the number of youngsters (mothers, children) who require services. The percentage of youth-gang members who are adolescent and young adult females isn't well defined. The number of young women who aren't hardcore gang members but nevertheless are affiliated to some degree with gang boys is also unknown. The number of children whose mothers are gang girls and fathers are gang boys is unknown. The number of gang boys who have abandoned children is unknown. And the quality of childcare delivered by gang-girl mothers or members of their extended families is unexamined in the gang literature.

Reaching Out to Gang Girls

Notwithstanding the ill-defined nature of this subpopulation, there are reasonable ways to reach out to gang girls. Finding them at school seems the easiest way, but Fremont research shows that hardcore girls who are most often pregnant and most involved in crime don't go to school. With this in mind, we can name a number of options. Communities can wait for them to be arrested. In 1995, 26 percent of juvenile arrests (adolescents under age 18) were females; although waiting for an arrest may be too late, this approach is better than doing nothing. Communities can reach out to juvenile females who seek medical care for pregnancy and related medical concerns at public hospitals. Communities can enlist the help of grassroots agencies. The Ad Hoc Group Against Crime (Ad Hoc), a long-standing privately and publicly funded outreach agency in Kansas City, Missouri, does an effective job of contacting kids in high-crime and gang neighborhoods. Ad Hoc's outreach workers are former gang members and adult offenders who have worked with neighborhood organizations, intervened in neighborhood household disputes, supported law enforcement efforts to stabilize high-crime neighborhoods, and saved dozens of young girls from sexual victimization by male gang members.

However, gang and drug detectives have the potential to be the most effective outreach workers. The dominant police role in Kansas City is crime suppression. That's important; however, there's more to policing than making arrests. Juvenile gangs and drug detectives have a moral, if not a legal, obligation to protect children from abuse and neglect and exposure to dangerous environments. Young children don't have to be black and blue for us to know they're in trouble; as long as their mothers are tied to gang boys, these kids are going to be in unhealthy environments.

The mother-child tie is a critical juncture, because it affords communities an intervention opportunity, which may slow the genesis of the next generation of young gang members and delinquents. Fremont research shows that a community's opportunity cost can be high when a gang or drug detective walks away from neglected children and adolescents and does nothing to intervene.

Supervised Residential Centers

Resources reallocated from juvenile and adult correctional budgets can support two types of supervised residential centers designed for adolescent gang-affiliated girls with or without children. The simpler center is a "safe house–working dormitory"; the more complex center is a "group home" for young mothers.

Residential centers should be located outside high-crime inner cities but close to high schools, community colleges, and jobs. A residential intervention offers girls an immediate change in the material conditions of their lives and gives them an opportunity to achieve independent living. Residential and financial independence is a dream of Fremont girls.

Formalizing local-level residential placements under federal oversight with financial contributions from counties, states, and the federal government, as well as corporations who'd hire these young women, would benefit everyone. Federal oversight may better ensure equity in the distribution of resources to the poorest communities. I am fearful that state- and local-elected officials may succumb to the pressure of voters who feel that repairing potholes, building a community swimming pool, and constructing a $60 million state prison are better options than supporting impoverished gang-affiliated girls and their babies.

Community leaders must ensure that the bureaucracy managing these residential centers is streamlined and consumes proportionately little of the allocated resources. Most important, supervisory staff should be trained managers who've passed careful background checks, including criminal history investigations, to ensure the physical and emotional safety of girls. Residential centers would be outstanding training centers for graduate students studying social work, criminal justice, family dynamics, and psychology.

Operations and Objectives

Generally speaking, supervised residential centers would operate on a consensual management model, which engages girls' cooperation with their social support and material gain. House rules and sanctions for violations should be a core underlying operational element, but threats of punishment must be kept in the background. Girls' program involvement and consensus in meeting house rules must be an outcome of their recognition of social support and material gain. Of course, there will be rule violations, but unless these are instances of serious violence, patience must be the order of the day until girls learn how to live in a rule-ordered environment. Gang boys must be kept out and curfews established. When gang boys discover that girls at residential centers have nothing of value to offer them, they will disappear.

Residential centers would meet three specific objectives: (1) to shelter and protect girls; (2) to provide education, job training, and job placement; and (3) to ensure a healthy start for gang girls' children. If gang girls aren't pregnant or already mothers, simple interventions, such as job training and placement, coupled with time to adjust to a new style of life may be all that's necessary to redirect them. However, both the intervention complexity and the opportunity cost increase dramatically when a teenage girl is pregnant or has a child. At that point, intervention must be designed for the immediate and long-term needs of mothers and children.

Fremont girls and their babies are illustrations of what happens when kids are reared on the street with inadequate adult supervision. If kids have no parents or adults who'll care for them, communities should become "surrogate" parents.

Safe House–Working Dormitory

The working poor suffer. An annual income of $10,000–$20,000 forces these wage earners to reside in cheap apartments in rundown neighborhoods far from good jobs in the suburbs. Cara's story shows what can happen when a single young woman who earns approximately $700 a month decides to share an apartment. True, she could have found a smaller, rattier apartment somewhere and lived alone, but that's not what a teenage girl actually does. True, she could have found a roommate other than Wendy [a fellow Fremont gang member] and kept the door closed in the face of drug-using and drug-selling companions. But these girls don't do that either. There's a lesson here: Communities should design programs on the basis of what gang girls do, not on what we wish they would do.

The first goal of safe houses–working dorms is to safeguard young girls by stabilizing them with housing, food, and safety in a communal residence. A communal lifestyle is an essential element in successful intervention. Dormitory life is more than housing. Girls need to have emotional security as well as social stability. These girls are scared of failure and have had few experiences in the mainstream world. Despite the bravado and street rhetoric, these girls are frightened, inexperienced children who need guidance and a group of companions to offer social and moral support.

The success of safe houses–working dorms may encourage more girls to leave the street. Cara's and Wendy's experiences on the job show that one girl can pull another one or two into the workplace. Cara and Wendy helped other Fremont gang members find work. The same energy and commitment these girls show toward drug selling can be diverted into staying straight if we provide them with basic support while they learn how to manage on their own.

Providing Stability

In a safe house, a girl can achieve stability and security. In this setting, she can be offered psychological and substance-abuse counseling. Kids who've been on the street need time to relax, settle down, learn to interact in positive ways, and most of all, "stay clean." A lifestyle of hanging out and using drugs keeps kids up all night and wears them out. Some Fremont kids disappeared for a week or two when they retreated to a safe spot to rest. Jail sometimes acts as a safe house. Once a young person adjusts to confinement, he or she adapts well and feels comfortable. [For example, during her stay at a detention center,] Cara ate regularly, slept all night, kept busy at productive activities all day, received drug and alcohol treatment, attended religious services, and went to school.

At Wendy and Cara's apartment, these girls' lives were monolithic, unproductive, and self-destructive, despite their working every day. By contrast, a safe house can be the first step in a multidimensional program delivery system and an alternative less costly than jails and detention centers.

Programs must include more than educational and counseling programs. Fremont kids have virtually no social ties of value to anyone outside the gang. Girls' ties to family members are strained, and a daughter-mother tie is valueless if the mother is a rock cocaine addict and an alcoholic.

A safe house can change a gang girl's social network by adding the ties she needs to the mainstream. Once girls sense that they're gaining more than they're losing, most of them will likely move to employment.

The second goal of safe houses–working dorms is to prepare girls with workplace skills. This can be accomplished with a careful assessment of a girl's strengths and weaknesses and the development of a detailed case management plan. For these girls, preparation for the workplace means more than acquiring job skills. They need basic social and language skills as well, because these have been cut short by inadequate family socialization, delinquency, and periods of isolation in detention centers and jails. . . .

Safe houses–working dorms are places where girls would receive vocational and social training and reside while they are working full-time at entry-level jobs. Girls would pay a portion of their income as room and board and do chores around the house. When these girls are stable and well trained in a variety of workplace skills, out-placement services could assist them in finding a decent apartment and a better job.

Group Homes for Young Mothers

Communities must face the issue of helping girls through pregnancy and the early years of motherhood. A low-paying job can't adequately support a young mother-to-be or meet the expenses of motherhood. Fremont research shows that gang girls live with economic and social poverty, and pregnancy makes that worse. . . .

What residential options are available within the personal social networks of pregnant, gang-affiliated girls or new mothers? The answer is, few. . . .

With a job earning minimum wage and no social ties to anyone who can economically support her, a pregnant girl or young mother is stuck on the street, forced to use welfare, and often is driven to open her doors to gang boys. . . .

Fremont research shows clearly that a pregnant teenage girl's life slowly and inevitably worsens. She's compelled to overcome: the reality of economic and social poverty and impending homelessness; social alienation from her family and perhaps also from her companions; recurring battles with her baby's father over financial and social support and his desire to "be with" other girls; and the physical and emotional discomfort of trips by bus to public health hospitals and long waits there, if she chooses to receive medical care. What's more, pregnancy puts social and financial pressure on the adult females in the mother-to-be's family. Often that pressure strains an already difficult relationship even more.

Community inaction in regard to this array of social problems has a catastrophic opportunity cost. The children of Fremont girls are the next generation of gangs like the Fremont Hustlers. Without community mobilization, I'm not sanguine about the prospects of a safe and healthy life for the other babies and preschoolers whose mothers hang on Fremont and 13th.

The single most important issue with the highest opportunity cost in youth-gang intervention is protecting babies and preschoolers. In gang-girl mothers' houses, young children are reared in economic and social, as well as moral, poverty. Engulfed in such a household, do these children have a reasonable opportunity to elude drugs and gangs? Only in a community's care will these children be protected.

In a group home, day care and an early-life program for children can get them off in the right direction while young mothers work and return home to a clean and protected environment where they learn how to help one another. Kansas City has new, low-income, single-family houses as well as apartments located in safe neighborhoods near downtown employment and along bus lines. When young women with and without children acquire more job skills and earn better incomes, they can be assisted in finding low-income housing and more sophisticated employment.

ORGANIZATIONS TO CONTACT

The editors have compiled the following list of organizations concerned with the issues presented in this book. The descriptions are derived from materials provided by the organizations. All have publications or information available for interested readers. The list was compiled on the date of publication of the present volume; the information provided here may change. Be aware that many organizations take several weeks or longer to respond to inquiries, so allow as much time as possible.

Boys and Girls Clubs of America
1230 W. Peachtree St. NW, Atlanta, GA 30309
(404) 487-5700
e-mail: LMclemore@bgca.org • website: www.bgca.org

Boys and Girls Clubs of America supports juvenile gang prevention programs in its individual clubs throughout the United States. The organization's Targeted Outreach program relies on referrals from schools, courts, law enforcement, and community youth service agencies to recruit at-risk youths into club programs and activities. It publishes *Gang Prevention Through Targeted Outreach*, a manual designed to assist local clubs in reaching young people before they become involved in gang activity.

Center for the Study and Prevention of Violence (CSPV)
Institute of Behavioral Science
University of Colorado at Boulder, Campus Box 439, Boulder, CO 80309-0439
(303) 492-8465 • fax: (303) 443-3297
e-mail: cspv@colorado.edu • website: www.colorado.edu/cspv

Founded in 1992, the CSPV assists groups in studying the causes of and prevention methods for youth violence and gang activity. The center's Information House compiles research literature relating to these problems and offers a database that is searchable by specific topic. In addition, the CSPV provides technical assistance to violence prevention groups and conducts in-house studies on the causes of youth violence.

Gang Crime Prevention Center (GCPC)
318 W. Adams St., 12th Fl., Chicago, IL 60606
(888) 411-4272
website: www.gcpc.state.il.us

Established in 1997, the GCPC provides the general public and law enforcement officials with technical assistance and a central repository of valuable information on gangs. Its four-tiered approach to gang prevention includes community mobilization, program development, research and information services, and operations. Together these units work to develop, implement, and evaluate both organizational and neighborhood-based gang prevention programs. The Program Network, GCPC's web-based repository, is the only online directory of programs addressing street gangs and the conditions that contribute to their growth and formation.

National Council on Crime and Delinquency (NCCD)
1970 Broadway, Suite 500, Oakland, CA 94612
(510) 208-0500 • fax: (510) 208-0511
e-mail: kxfisher@chorus.net • website: www.nccd-crc.org

The NCCD assists government, law enforcement, and community organizations in developing programs to address juvenile justice and gang problems. It conducts research, promotes reform initiatives, and works to prevent and reduce juvenile crime and delinquency. The council publishes the informational booklet *Reducing Crime in America: A Pragmatic Approach.*

National Crime Prevention Council (NCPC)
1000 Connecticut Ave. NW, 13th Fl., Washington, DC 20036
(202) 466-6272 • fax: (202) 296-1356
website: www.ncpc.org

The council works to prevent juvenile crime and to build safer neighborhoods. Its Youth as Resources program, which encourages local youngsters to implement projects to help their communities, is based on the premise that young people have the desire and capability to address many youth crime problems on their own. The council's publications include two information packets, *Helping Youth with Gang Prevention* and *Tools to Involve Parents in Gang Prevention.*

National Gang Crime Research Center (NGCRC)
PO Box 990, Peotone, IL 60468-0990
(708) 258-9111 • fax: (773) 995-3819
e-mail: gangcrime@aol.com • website: www.ngcrc.com

Formed in 1990, the NGCRC conducts research on gangs and gang members, disseminates information through publications and reports, and provides training and consulting services. On its website, the center makes available its national survey research reports studying the relationship of gangs and the economy, prisons, and guns. It also publishes the quarterly *Journal of Gang Research.*

National Major Gang Task Force (NMGTF)
338 S. Arlington Ave., Indianapolis, IN 46219
(317) 322-0537 • fax: (317) 322-0549
e-mail: nmgtf@earthlink.net • website: www.nmgtf.org

The NMGTF's goal is to provide a centralized link for all fifty state correctional systems, the Federal Bureau of Prisons, major jails, law enforcement, and probation and parole offices throughout the nation. The task force accomplishes this mission by generating and maintaining the National Correction Informational Sharing System, which is available to gang prevention groups across the country. It publishes the monograph "From the Street to the Prison: Understanding and Responding to Gangs."

National School Safety Center (NSSC)
141 Duesenberg Dr., Suite 11, Westlake Village, CA 91362
(805) 373-9977 • fax: (805) 373-9277
e-mail: info@nssc1.org • website: www.nssc1.org

The NSSC's mission is to train educators, law enforcement officers, and other youth-serving professionals in school crime prevention and safe school planning. The center also provides on-site technical assistance to school districts and conducts safety site assessments to help schools with crime prevention. Its many publications include the book *Gangs in Schools: Breaking Up Is Hard to Do* and the newsletter *School Safety Update*, which is published nine times a year.

National Youth Gang Center (NYGC)
Institute for Intergovernmental Research
PO Box 12729, Tallahassee, FL 32317
(850) 385-0600 • fax (850) 386-5356
e-mail: nygc@iir.com • website: www.iir.com/nygc

The purpose of the NYGC is to expand and maintain the body of critical knowledge about youth gangs and effective responses to them. The center assists state and local jurisdictions in the collection, analysis, and exchange of information on gang-related demographics, legislation, literature, research, and promising program strategies. Among its publications are *The NYGC Bibliography of Gang Literature* and the papers "A Comprehensive Response to America's Youth Gang Problem" and "Gang Suppression and Intervention: Problem and Response."

Office of Juvenile Justice and Delinquency Prevention (OJJDP)
810 Seventh St. NW, Washington, DC 20531
(202) 307-5911 • fax: (202) 307-2093
e-mail: askjj@ncjrs.org • website: http://ojjdp.ncjrs.org

As the primary federal agency charged with monitoring and improving the juvenile justice system, the OJJDP provides national leadership, coordination, and resources in the prevention of juvenile delinquency and victimization. The organization also works to improve the juvenile justice system so that it better protects the public safety, holds offenders accountable, and provides treatment and rehabilitative services for delinquent juveniles. The OJJDP publishes the annual *National Youth Gang Survey*, as well as the bulletins "Gang Members and Delinquent Behavior," "Youth Gangs: An Overview," and "The Youth Gangs, Drugs, and Violence Connection."

BIBLIOGRAPHY

Books

Curtis W. Branch
Clinical Interventions with Gang Adolescents and Their Families. Boulder, CO: Westview Press, 1997.

Curtis W. Branch, ed.
Adolescent Gangs: Old Issues, New Approaches. Philadelphia, PA: Brunner/Mazel, 1999.

Meda Chesney-Lind and John M. Hagedorn, eds.
Female Gangs in America: Essays on Girls, Gangs, and Gender. Chicago: Lake View Press, 1999.

Ko-lin Chin
Chinatown Gangs: Extortion, Enterprise, and Ethnicity. New York: Oxford University Press, 1996.

Herbert C. Covey, Scott Menard, and Robert J. Franzese
Juvenile Gangs. Springfield, IL: Charles C. Thomas, 1997.

G. David Curry and Scott H. Decker
Confronting Gangs: Crime and Community. Los Angeles: Roxbury Park, 2002.

Scott H. Decker and Barrik Van Winkle
Life in the Gang: Family, Friends, and Violence. New York: Cambridge University Press, 1996.

Arnold P. Goldstein and Donald W. Kodluboy
Gangs in Schools: Signs, Symbols, and Solutions. Champaign, IL: Research Press, 1998.

John M. Hagedorn
People and Folks: Gangs, Crime, and the Underclass in a Rustbelt City. Chicago: Lake View Press, 1997.

Arturo Hernandez
Peace in the Streets: Breaking the Cycle of Gang Violence. Washington, DC: Child Welfare League of America, 1998.

James C. Howell
Youth Gangs: An Overview. Washington, DC: U.S. Department of Justice, 1998.

C. Ronald Huff
Criminal Behavior of Gang Members and At-Risk Youths. Washington, DC: U.S. Department of Justice, 1998.

C. Ronald Huff, ed.
Gangs in America III. Thousand Oaks, CA: Sage, 2001.

Karen L. Kinnear
Gangs: A Reference Handbook. Santa Barbara, CA: ABC-CLIO, 1996.

George W. Knox
An Introduction to Gangs. Peotone, IL: New Chicago School Press, 2000.

G. Larry Mays, ed.
Gangs and Gang Behavior. Chicago: Nelson-Hall, 1997.

Joan McCord, ed.
Violence and Childhood in the Inner City. New York: Cambridge University Press, 1997.

Daniel J. Monti
Wannabe: Gangs in Suburbs and Schools. Cambridge, MA: Blackwell, 1994.

Chester G. Oehme III
Gangs, Groups, and Crime: Perceptions and Responses of Community Organizations. Durham, NC: Carolina Academic Press, 1997.

Susan A. Phillips — *Wallbangin': Graffiti and Gangs in L.A.* Chicago: University of Chicago Press, 1999.

Fred Rosen — *Gang Mom.* New York: St. Martin's, 1998.

Randall G. Shelden, Sharon K. Tracy, and William B. Brown — *Youth Gangs in American Society.* Belmont, CA: Wadsworth, 2001.

James F. Short Jr. — *Gangs and Adolescent Violence.* Boulder, CO: Center for the Study and Prevention of Violence, 1996.

Gini Sikes — *Eight Ball Chicks: A Year in the Violent World of Girl Gangsters.* New York: Anchor Books, 1997.

Irving A. Spergel — *The Youth Gang Problem: A Community Approach.* New York: Oxford University Press, 1995.

Gail B. Stewart — *Gangs.* San Diego, CA: Lucent Books, 1997.

Mark D. Totten — *Guys, Gangs, and Girlfriend Abuse.* Orchard Park, NY: Broadview Press, 2000.

Valerie Wiener — *Winning the War Against Youth Gangs: A Guide for Teens, Families, and Communities.* Westport, CT: Greenwood Press, 1999.

Periodicals

Tom Batsis — "Helping Schools Respond to Gang Violence," *Journal of Gang Research*, Spring 1997. Available from the National Gang Crime Research Center, PO Box 990, Peotone, IL 60468-0990, or at www.ngcrc.com/ngcrc/page2.htm.

Tim Cornwell — "L.A.'s Most Wanted," *Los Angeles Times Educational Supplement*, March 17, 2000.

Nancy De Los Santos — "LAPD Crusades Against Homies," *Hispanic*, December 1999. Available from Hispanic Publishing Corporation, 999 Ponce de Leon Blvd., Suite 600, Coral Gables, FL 33134, or at www.hispanicmagazine.com.

John J. DiIulio Jr. — "How to Defuse the Youth Crime Bomb," *Weekly Standard*, March 10, 1996. Available from 1150 17th St. NW, Suite 505, Washington, DC 20036, or at www.weeklystandard.com/search/search.asp.

Economist — "Gangs in the Heartland," May 25–31, 1996.

Blaine Harden — "Boston's Approach to Juvenile Crime Encircles Youths, Reduces Slayings," *Washington Post*, October 23, 1997. Available from Reprints, 1150 15th St. NW, Washington, DC 20071, or at www.washingtonpost.com/wp-adv./archives/front.htm.

Ross Howard — "A Child's Garden of Dope: Vietnamese Gangs Make Cultivating Marijuana a Family Affair," *Maclean's*, April 3, 2000.

Edward Humes — "Can a Gang Girl Go Straight?" *Glamour*, March 1996.

Arleen Jacobius — "Court Approves Gang Injunctions," *ABA Journal*, April 1997.

Journal of Gang Research	"The Facts About Female Gang Members," Spring 1997.
George W. Knox	"Crips: A Gang Profile Analysis," *Journal of Gang Research*, Spring 1997.
John A. Laskey	"The Gang Snitch Profile," *Journal of Gang Research*, Spring 1997.
John Leland	"Savior of the Streets," *Newsweek*, June 1, 1998.
Steve Lopez	"The Mutant Brady Bunch: Meet Salt Lake City's Clean-Cut, Anti-Drug Street Gang—and Tremble," *Time*, August 30, 1999.
Courtland Milloy	"Truce Leads Gang Members to New Lives," *Washington Post*, November 9, 1997.
Fen Montaigne	"Deporting America's Gang Culture," *Mother Jones*, July/August 1999.
National Gang Crime Research Center	"The Gang Dictionary: A Guide to Gang Slang, Gang Vocabulary, and Gang Socio-Linguistic Phrases," *Journal of Gang Research*, Summer 1997.
Fernando Parra	"A Street Gang in Fact," *Journal of Gang Research*, Spring 1997.
John H. Richardson	"The Latin Kings Play Songs of Love," *New York*, February 17, 1997.
Lucas Rivera	"Latin King Tries to Change Image," *Hispanic*, June 1997.
Nancy Jo Sales	"Teenage Gangland," *New York*, December 16, 1996.
David G. Savage	"Civil Liberties Back on the Street: Anti-Gang Efforts Struck Down," *ABA Journal*, August 1999.
Douglas Stanglin	"New Gang in Town," *U.S. News & World Report*, October 13, 1997.
Nancy Stein	"The Gang Truce: A Movement for Social Justice: An Interview with Michael Zinzun," *Social Justice*, Winter 1997.
Darryl Van Duch	"Anti-Gang Law a Loitering Ban?" *National Law Journal*, April 6, 1998. Available from 105 Madison Ave., New York, NY 10016, or at www.nlj.com.
Michelle Wagner, Carla Knudsen, and Victoria Harper	"The Evil Joker: Open Discussion Helps Students Examine the Dangers of Gangs," *Educational Leadership*, December 1999/January 2000. Available from the Association for Supervision and Curriculum Development, 1703 N. Beauregard St., Alexandria, VA 22311, or at www.ascd.org.

INDEX